Girl With a Suitcase

JACQUELINE COX

Copyright © 2019 Jacqueline Cox

This is a limited edition, produced for the friends and family of the author

Published by Jacqueline Cox in the UK

Designed by:
Book of My Life Ltd
15 Keynote Studios
62–72 Dalmain Road
London
SE23 1AT
020 8133 6588
bookofmylife.co.uk

Book of My Life

This book is for my children, Kelly, Steve, Sheena and Danny. Also for Derek, my soulmate.

The story is told as I remember it. However, I have changed a few names to protect the innocent.

Prologue

Dead.

She's dead.

One week after my sixteenth birthday, one month before my final exams, my guardian had died.

I was now homeless. And I felt like an orphan.

I blinked through damp lashes at the shiny brass plaque screwed to the wooden lid of the box that held my grandmother's body.

Kathleen Jennifer Tabor 1894–1956

Edging closer to the wooden plinth cradling the coffin, I slid my hand along the smooth rim of the white satin lining. As my grandmother's head came into view, I gasped. I hadn't known what to expect. How could I? It was the first time I had seen a dead body.

A soft fringe of crimped, greying hair framed my grandmother's face. She doesn't look that old, I thought, noticing how smooth her skin was. Hardly any wrinkles. She looks half her age.

Poor Gran. It was bad timing you going like that.

My grandmother looked like she was sleeping. I half expected to see her eyelids lift and her piercing blue eyes look straight back at me.

Nobody had made me come here. Who was there to now that Gran was gone? My curiosity had got the better of me, that's all.

Sinking to my knees on a hassock beneath the alabaster carving of an angel, I clasped my hands, closed my eyes and began to murmur the Lord's Prayer. It was Gran who had taught me the invocation when I was little.

Then looking around, I noticed the chapel of rest and walked inside. It was a small oblong room with white painted walls dotted with gold-framed pictures depicting garden scenes. Gran would have liked that. A pair of wicker-seated high-backed chairs stood against the wall; three long tapers flickered; a bowl of white fragrant lilies sat on a small wooden table in one corner. An air of serenity engulfed the small room and me with it.

Suddenly the door burst open. I swung round and came face to face with the person on earth I hated most: Aunt Peggy. Hair immaculate as always. A little older now, thicker lipstick and mascara. But yes, the same Aunt Peggy.

"What do you think you're doing here?" she demanded, in her highfalutin voice. "Children are not allowed."

"Hello Auntie. I know that, but I'm 16 now," I replied proudly, determined not to be intimidated now that I had reached that magical age.

"That's as maybe," hissed the woman in black. "But as far as I'm concerned, you're still a child."

She squawked again, roughly squeezing my arm and shoving me towards the doorway. "Come here!" Her voice vibrated around the walls.

My aunt's expression darkened further.

"Ouch, you're hurting me!" I cried, wincing as her sharp, red talons cut into my flesh through the thin sleeve of my new floral lawn dress.

Instinctively, my arms rose up in defence, but my aunt persisted with her attack, scratching at me like a demented cat.

"You little bitch!" she hissed, pulling out a clump of my dark hair.

I resisted the temptation to fight back, though the sap rose in my breast. There were old scores to settle. But not today, not with my grandmother so close.

"Get out, you horrible child!" she wailed. "You killed her!"

Her voice rose. She had no control over it nor of her temper. She spat and grabbed hold of me, pushing me so hard out of the door of the chapel of rest that I caught my heel and ended up sprawled across the marble floor. The door slammed shut behind me.

It was just like her to make a fuss, and at Gran's funeral as well. She hasn't changed, I thought. Still as hateful as ever.

And hate her I did.

I managed to stand up and dust myself down, noticing a spot of blood on my sleeve.

Wiping a tear from my cheek, I felt a tingling sensation surge through my body while my aunt's last words whirled around inside my brain.

You killed her.

As I dabbed my arm with one of Gran's monogrammed handkerchiefs, I heard a softer voice at my shoulder.

"All right, girl?"

I had no trouble recognising Uncle Rob and his soothing, gentle lilt. How could I forget this loveable, kind man? How on earth could he be married to that woman?

"Sure," I lied, "just caught me arm on the door."

Banging his pipe on the sole of his shoe, fingering

his brown moustache, Uncle Rob's puzzled expression suddenly dissipated, as though he had solved some great mystery.

"Why, it's little Jacqueline isn't it?" he said.

A crowd was now encircling me.

"My, just look at you, all grown up! The last time I saw you, you were knee high to a grasshopper.

"Have you seen your Aunt Peggy?"

I thought it wise not to mention the scuffle.

"She's in the chapel of rest," I replied meekly, pointing to the wooden door.

"Oh, is she? Ah well, perhaps I won't disturb her then," he said. "After all, Kitty was her mother."

His face broke out into that familiar wicked grin. "Let's go and find the others, shall we?"

Strolling arm in arm with the witch's husband along the narrow, carpeted corridor to join the assembled relatives, I felt happier inside, more secure. I wondered if I would see my younger sister at the funeral but immediately dismissed the thought, recalling my aunt's words: Children not allowed. My sister was two years younger than me. I desperately wanted to ask my uncle about her but decided against the idea, not wishing to upset him. Not today of all days.

Nudging the glazed swing door open with my good arm, I stepped into the warm May sunshine. A breeze gently kissed my flushed cheeks.

The family huddled together near the hearse.

"Look who's here!" Uncle Rob clasped my hand gently, edging me towards my relatives. I searched the sea of faces, vaguely remembering some of the aunts and uncles, my grandmother's children, seven in total: three girls, four boys (two a set of twins).

With one hand shielding my eyes from the bright sunlight, I was surprised and delighted to spot a familiar figure sitting on a wooden bench next to the rose arbour.

Heart beating, I ran towards Gran's eldest child—my mum.

I flopped down beside her, putting an arm around her shoulders in an attempt at comfort. She shrugged it off. At first I felt hurt but quickly remembered that Mum could not be held responsible for her actions.

Not wishing to cause her any further concern, my head still pounding, I covered my wound with grubby gloves, hoping she would not notice. I longed to be able to lift her spirits.

"Glad you made it, Mum," was all I could manage.

It was a miracle Joan was there. My mother suffered deep bouts of depression, swallowing a cocktail of tablets just to get through the day.

"Had one of me heads, Jackie," she said. "Feel a bit better now I've had a pill."

I just wanted to hug her but thought better of it. She looked so fragile, as if she might break. Her clothes, a creased black skirt and a black lacy long-sleeved top, had seen better days. Her hair had been shoved inelegantly under a black cloche hat.

Mum used to be so particular about the way she looked.

"You look nice, Mum."

"Well, black's black."

I couldn't argue with that.

"Time to go, Mum." I helped my mother to her feet, tucking an arm through my own, supporting her as much as possible. Together, we slowly made our way towards the waiting black limousines and the small group of mourners.

"Come on, old girl," Uncle Rob came forward to help his eldest sister-in-law into the car. Then "Look who's here," he said, pushing his wife in front of me.

Taken by surprise, I stepped backwards, not sure what to say, but my fears soon dispersed as Aunt Peggy turned on the charm for the benefit of her audience.

"Well, Jacqueline, you have grown. Quite the young lady now."

Lines of hatred were etched around her lips, which were pursed, daring me to mention our earlier encounter.

I smiled softly, following my mother, aunt and uncle into the waiting car.

"Where're we going, Mum?"

Before my mother could answer, Aunt Peggy's authoritative voice cut in.

"The cortege will proceed to the crematorium, Joan, then on to our Uncle Fred's place for refreshments."

Later that day, in the sanctuary of my small bedroom, alone with my thoughts, my guardian at rest, I wondered who would now answer all the questions ferrying through my mind.

One thing was certain: I would soon be packing my tatty old brown suitcase yet again.

Destination unknown.

Chapter 1
The Firstborn of a Firstborn

As heavy bombers laboured across the dark heavens northward, my mother laboured down below. I arrived on earth unable to compete with the noise overhead. The weather, on 28 April 1941 in Fareham, Hampshire, was dry, dull and rather cold. My arrival was badly timed. Air-raid sirens wailed while the pantry became a makeshift delivery room.

Being born is hard enough, but being the firstborn of a firstborn also brings many expectations. Being loved is one. Though, of course, as children we do not know this; we only know what we experience.

Growing up in war-torn Britain of the 1940s, my mother, the first of seven, lived with her parents and siblings in a large red-brick house alongside my grandfather's business. He was a master baker in Shenfield. My father and a few uncles in the forces were away at war when I arrived.

Initially, I was a source of joy and diversion to my mother and grandparents. Soon I learned to mount the rickety, wooden steps to the back of the bakery for fresh rolls, chewing happily on a warm crust, the sweet scent of yeast enveloping me.

Granddad ran two delivery vans and two horses and carts. After the birth of my sister, I became more distant from my mother and spent more time with my aunts, delivering bread and cakes to local customers.

While accompanying an aunt in a van one day, the vehicle swerved around a corner on the road towards Shenfield station, flinging me out. They said I was lucky to survive, and I wonder now why I did. Gran, who was religious, believed God had saved me. Mum insisted the M&B tablets had something to do with it.

Going down to the air-raid shelter became a great adventure for us children. The adults did not share our enthusiasm. Gran spouted: "Why does the devil get his own way?" On one occasion we didn't make the shelter in time, and as aircraft thundered over our houses, I grabbed my little sister and pulled her under the large refectory table. An entire terrace of four was demolished. Our house and bakery remained intact.

Lucky again! (What is it that they say? Cats have nine lives.)

One day, when Dad came home in his uniform, we moved. Mum, Dad and us two girls, all my worldly belongings packed into a tattered old brown suitcase. Home became a Nissen hut situated in a camp in a field. A long, steel tube-like construction, the hut was divided into rooms by curtains, which Mum felt would give privacy and warmth. A small garden surrounded the building. There Mum hung washing and I played. Gran visited fairly often, bringing food, whatever she could spare on rations.

Soon after a street party celebrating the end of the war, we moved again, the four of us with Dad no longer in uniform. My suitcase came with us, of course. It was a terraced house in a proper street: two up, two down, inside toilet, blue front door, small garden out back, an even smaller one at the front. It was located near a railway line, walking distance from school. Mum loved it, but I missed the carpets in Granddad's house. Lino felt cold to small bare feet. No socks allowed indoors. Strictly for wearing out.

Mum and Dad began to argue. Dad found it hard to settle down and adjust after leaving the forces. Us girls didn't really know him.

So I packed up my little suitcase and we moved again, this time to a farmhouse in the country (Great Leighs) called Domley Cottage. This I thought a great place to live with lots of rooms, or so it seemed to me. The house contained passages and cupboards ideal for hide and seek.

I watched in awe the day the combine harvester came in. With the weather hot and sunny, this strange machine encircled the large field until a small square remained in the centre. Two men, one being my father, aimed shotguns and fired into the wheat. What seemed like hundreds of rabbits scattered in all directions. Pie for dinner? Not today. These creatures had myxomatosis. I felt sad for those that didn't get away and watched as they were scraped up into the back of a truck.

I've never eaten rabbit again.

The woods near the cottage were perfect for exploring and foraging. One day I picked a basketful of mushrooms, proudly carrying my discovery back to the cottage for tea. Mum became ill in the night. I was scolded for trying to poison her.

During a bad storm one night, Mum was locked out and banged on the door, waking me up. When Dad opened the door, Mum was illuminated by the lightning, soaking wet, stomach bulging. Shortly after that night Dad went away. No one said where. No one mentioned it.

A short while later Gran visited and left with my sister. Was it something I had done? Was it the mushroom episode? No one explained. Children had to be seen and not heard.

Mum spent her days crying and taking pills. My questions hung unanswered.

A short while later, maybe days, maybe weeks, Gran came for me. Mum stood on the doorstep as Gran carried my battered old brown suitcase containing all my belongings. No one hugged me. No one kissed me goodbye. No one waved.

A new chapter in my life began.

Chapter 2
The Three Js

Gran's ground-floor flat, in a block of eight, became my new home. I hunted everywhere for my little sister, but she was nowhere to be seen; it was just Gran and me.

Situated in an alleyway off Brentwood High Street near King's Road, which leads down to the railway station, it was a small flat with two bedrooms, a living room, kitchen, inside bathroom and outdoor toilet. *Paul Temple* spawned my love of detective stories. I'd be all ears listening to the series on Gran's Bush radio. One neighbour next door let me play with Billy, her little dog. Gran had a bike which I learned to ride, although I couldn't reach the saddle; it was much too high for a five year old.

It's funny, as a child you just accept things the way they are. It wasn't until a few years later that I began to wonder where the rest of my family were living. I had learned not to ask questions. Maybe that's why today I ask so many, sometimes to people's annoyance.

Being an only child now, I soon learned to play on my own. I never got too close to anyone nor too friendly as I believed they might just disappear. At that young age I made a rule not to form friendships, not to talk too much, definitely not to love. Not that I really understood what love was, not then anyway.

Summertime passed with regular visits to cousins and aunts, which always made me happy. The summer of 1947 was the sixth warmest on record.

Then, on a day in early September, I found my old brown suitcase on my bed. Gran informed me that I was going to stay at a school. I broke the rule and asked for how long. She just looked at me and mumbled something about living there.

Here we go again.

Carrying my bulging, tatty suitcase, I caught a train (a great thrill) to London with Gran, arriving at the school in Hertfordshire in time for tea.

On arrival, someone grabbed my suitcase from Gran with one hand and steered me away with the other.

No goodbyes, no hugs, no kisses.

I was ushered into a large room (later I learned it was called a dormitory) with eight white metal-framed beds topped with white counterpanes. After being allocated a bed, I was told to unpack.

You would think I had become accustomed to being uprooted suddenly. In a way I was. But this was different. This time I was with strangers, with no one to relate to—quite daunting for a six year old. Years later, I learned that Gran felt she couldn't handle me any longer; I had become too 'feisty'.

I thought I was normal.

I soon began to communicate with my roommates, and midnight feasts became regular occurrences. Older girls crept downstairs to the pantry for bread-and-dripping sandwiches. The congealed fat at the bottom of the roasting tray, eaten with salt, became a favourite.

My education continued. School was a two-mile walk away. Some of us found a short cut through the playground of a senior school, although we were frequently chased away by the big kids. For fun we often climbed the steep grassy embankment of the nearby railway line to the single track above the bridge, only to slide down the other side. Being a branch line we never saw any trains. But one very cold morning during our usual dare over the rail track, the bank was icy. I slipped somehow, managing to get my foot wedged. The others tried pulling me free but to no avail. In the distance the hoot of a steam train could be heard. It was late due to a hold-up because of the bad weather. Sitting on the sleepers in between the tracks, I could feel the vibration on the rails. I had a feeling that this would be my end.

"We'll get you out," Jimmy kept yelling while he and Jenny pulled. I wriggled and wriggled my foot, which suddenly shot free leaving behind my school shoe, now broken. I had to walk the rest of the way to school without it.

Because of this escapade, the three of us arrived late for assembly. Mrs Darley (whom everyone feared) was waiting for us in the locker room, where I was attempting to put my plimsolls on.

Whenever we were late, and unfortunately that was quite often, we were commanded to hold out our hands to be smacked several times with a black plimsoll. Today was no exception. Both Jenny and I suffered the plimsoll assault, the sole of the shoe stinging our already cold hands. Jimmy, being a boy, received the missile around his cheeks. Today the force seemed stronger as the weapon struck our small hands, making tears well up in our eyes. I had learned not to cry. Poor Jimmy was left with a weal across his right cheek. She had gone too far this time. Soon the rest of the staff knew about it and immediate action was taken. Mrs Darley was dismissed. We children said she was expelled.

During two months of hard-packed winter snow, the school never closed. Each morning in assembly, before the head spoke, we listened to the hymn 'Morning has Broken'.

Halfway through April a maypole was erected on the grass, and we were given lessons on how to weave in and out and not bump into each other. The maypole was a tall, wooden pole with coloured ribbons, mainly red, green and blue, dangling from the top. We stood in twos and were instructed to face the same direction with a ribbon in our right hand. There was to be no overtaking. It took many lessons to perfect the art of weaving in and out (over and under) as we had to skip, but some of us wanted to run and kept bumping into each other and going the wrong way, sometimes on purpose. The ribbons became tangled, so back to the beginning. Once we had mastered the plait, the unwinding began. This caused even more confusion. If we got it wrong, we were threatened with losing our place on the maypole team. Our performance was to be at the Royal Albert Hall and we didn't want to miss that. Eventually we got it right in time for the festival. We travelled to London on a green Bedford coach which suffered a puncture on the way. Excitement onboard had never been so high. Our costumes were packed into wicker crates: gingham dresses and black patent shoes with red bows for the girls; shorts and gingham shirts for the boys. On arrival at the Royal Albert Hall, we were shown into a large dressing room with many other children from different schools. Halfway through our routine, I began to hobble as my feet hurt. The whole performance stopped: music, dance, everything. Someone grabbed my arm. My black patent shoes were removed and another pair put on. Apparently I was wearing the wrong ones. The music resumed. We dancers resumed. The audience clapped. I cried.

Housework became ingrained in me while at this school. Every Saturday morning, my chore was cleaning the hallway floor. This I looked forward to. I would skate across the wooden floorboards. To me the floor was ice and the dusters tied around my feet, my skates.

One chore I did not relish: polishing cutlery and laying it out uniformly on a table for inspection. Mrs Salter often made me redo forks as the polish still clung between the prongs.

I soon learned that housework definitely *was* a chore and had to be done no matter what.

The housework was worth suffering as on Saturday afternoons we were allowed to visit the local sweet shop, located at the foot of the hill. Clutching our ration coupon (16oz per month) and pennies, we would choose our favourite treats. Mine were aniseed balls, bulls' eyes and liquorice. My money never stretched to chocolate. Perhaps that is why I like it too much today.

Our dormitory was on the ground floor. One night, an intruder managed to break in. We screamed and screamed and screamed. From then on our dormitory was on first floor. Even today, I do not like sleeping at street level.

Sunday morning attendance at church was compulsory, part of our weekly routine. The only problem encountered, along with Jenny and Jimmy, were black lips after scrumping in the vicar's garden, which rather gave the game away. The three of us had several private audiences with the vicar and missed out on our Saturday sweet treats.

One escapade that earned disapproval from adults happened on a sunny day. The 'Three Js', as we called ourselves, decided to run away. Leaving the coop without any luggage (well we couldn't take any—people would be suspicious) we made our way towards the town, which was a few miles away. By teatime we all began to feel hungry with no food and no money. Jimmy came up with the idea of begging, which proved fruitless. As time progressed, we did not. Next idea: Jimmy knocked on a door, telling the lady who answered that he had become separated from his Cub pack and needed money to buy food. The lady invited him in while us girls hid behind the hedge. She then became suspicious and called the police. As the squad car turned up, we knew our adventure was over. The policeman shepherded us into the back of the police car. No one said a word. No one shouted. The officer drove us back to school, where we were met by Miss Salter, who quickly steered us, with rumbling tummies, towards the kitchen and food. Sheer heaven.

We scoffed until we were full.

End of term loomed, and a few weeks later everyone went home for the holidays.

But I didn't just go home for the holiday. I left, never to return.

It turned out that my part in the running away was more serious than I had realised. Three missing children was simply not acceptable. Rules are rules—not to be abused.

I had been expelled.

Chapter 3
Southampton Docks

The last time I held my sister Susan's hand we were standing on the dock at Southampton. She was four years old and I was six.

"Jackie, wake up!"

My grandmother was gently shaking me awake.

I opened my eyes. "What's wrong?"

"We're going to see Susan off today," she said quietly. The bed was still warm and inviting, but the thought of seeing my younger sister again sent me throwing back the bed covers enthusiastically.

Our father had shouted a lot before walking out. Mum fell apart. Us girls liked it when he went away. Mum didn't, confessing in one quiet moment that she still loved him and missed him terribly.

Trying to cope with two small children and another on the way proved too much for her. The baby was born, a third daughter. She lived with Mum for a few months. Then one day she was no longer around. Nobody explained where she had gone or why. Mum, still grieving, sought what little comfort she could in the safety of her nursing world. She lived and worked in a nearby hospital while I stayed with Gran, and Susan moved in with our mother's sister and brother-in-law. (I found this out later; nobody told me.)

"Where's she going, Gran?" Curiosity filled me up. I thought she might be going on one of Auntie's shopping trips.

"Oh, a long way from here," said Gran. "To the other side of the world. To foreign parts. You know, abroad."

"Is she going on a plane, Gran?"

"No, but I don't see why not. Your Uncle Rob works for BOAC. It must be quicker and cheaper to fly. But you know your Aunt Peggy. Probably thinks the sea voyage will do them good."

That morning the journey held a new kind of magic for me. It was the first time I had travelled by steam train. Boarding the 7:33am from Brentwood station, two travellers—one big one small—jostled with white starched collars, black rolled up umbrellas and bowler hats.

We were lucky to get seats although not window ones, which disappointed me as I really wanted to watch the world whizz by. Instead I watched the other passengers: men reading *The Times* and *Punch* having bought them at the platform's newsstand; women knitting or chatting. Listening to the grinding noise as the wheels ran along the tracks, I closed my eyes and was in a *Paul Temple* episode with the Coronation Scot steaming through the night to somewhere exotic.

Soon the train reached the buffers at Liverpool Street station, and eager travellers filed through the ticket barrier.

"Gran, I need the toilet."

"Oh, you're always wanting to go somewhere!" Grabbing my hand, she marched forwards. "Come on then."

A rush of passengers swept us towards the ladies and down the steps deep beneath WH Smith, where we found the entrance to the turnstile completely blocked by a rather oversized lady. After reclaiming her spinning coin from the newly washed floor, she was endeavouring to ease her ample frame into the narrow opening. Somehow in the gush of activity, a Co-op plastic carrier bag had become trapped, showering peanuts over the now impatient queue behind her. Four desperate females formed a scrum and slammed into the incredible bulk, sending the metal bars forward. As her hips passed through, the bars squeezed together and she shot free like a bar of wet soap—to everyone's relief.

Back above ground, I headed with Gran towards the tube.

"Which way now, Jackie?" uttered a bewildered Gran, searching the large coloured map on the wall. "My eyes aren't so good these days." (She always insisted she didn't need glasses.) I chose the green route, so we walked through the tunnel, accompanied by people heading to their places of work in the City.

On the escalator, the draught suddenly lifted Gran's new wide-brimmed hat. It hovered a few inches above her head before taking off on another gust, like a flying saucer gyrating into space.

"Quick, me hat!"

"All right, Gran. I'll get it."

I turned, forcing my way back up the crowded escalator only to see a surprised City gent catching the hat full in the face, causing him to lose his footing. Arms, legs and briefcase went flying as he parted company with his bowler hat and umbrella.

"Thanks mister." Snatching the hat I made a fast getaway, hanging on to it as though my life depended upon it.

"Knew I needed a new hatpin," Gran sighed, wiping her eye with the back of her hand and gently dusting the hat down, relieved to take back possession of the headpiece having spent weeks crafting it, sewing on wax fruit and fabric flowers to create the desired summery effect.

When at last we reached Waterloo mainline station, we joined the queue for third-class tickets. Glancing about I watched, in amazement, porters balancing luggage on barrows larger than them.

"Gran, I'm hungry."

"You're always hungry, child. You'll have to wait till you get on the train." I knew what she meant. A well-stocked picnic basket always accompanied Gran on excursions. That was one thing she excelled at.

Once Gran had the tickets, we passed through the barrier to board the steam locomotive. I could hardly contain my excitement at seeing the shiny coaches. We passed first class with blue curtains drawn as smoke already spiralled from the smokestack. The guard blew his whistle and waved his green flag. Happily I settled down on the crowded, noisy train, munching my way through home-made Cornish pasties and cakes, this time gazing out from a window seat. *Diddly dum diddly dee, diddly dum diddly dee* the wheels sang on the tracks as we rattled along, watching in awe as back gardens rushed by, and I thought of where I had lived when younger: cows, horses and sheep grazing in rolling buttercup fields; trees swaying gently on green landscapes. The countryside would always hold a place in my heart.

But, like all young children, I soon became bored with the view.

"Gran, can I go for a walk?"

"All right," sighed Gran, glancing up from her *Woman's Own,* "but only along the corridor and back. No further mind you."

I was glad to be out of the overcrowded compartment. It had become hot and stuffy, with a bearded man sitting in the corner incessantly puffing and sucking on his pipe, much to everyone's annoyance.

Once outside it seemed like another world in the busy corridor: Passengers walking backwards and forwards, leaning on brass rails attached to the windows, talking and laughing. Further along the corridor a boy and girl, about my age, chased each other, weaving in and out of holidaymakers, day trippers, men and women in forces' uniform with kitbags.

The boy stopped and stared at me.

"Want to play?"

"Come on, Tom," called the girl, running off. "Your turn to catch me!"

The invitation too good to refuse, I tagged along behind, following Tom, who suddenly stopped, scratching his head.

"Don't know where she's gone. Spect she's playing hide and seek. We always end up playing that."

"I'll help you find her," I offered, the spirit of adventure rising inside me. I darted along the busy corridor with Tom, searching for his sister, not noticing how far along the train I had travelled but suddenly realising it must be a long way from Gran.

Entering the dark guard's van, objects loomed in the dim light. I twisted my ankle. Tom and his sister were nowhere to be seen. Then a glare from a torchlight shone in my frightened face.

"Eh, wot you doing in 'ere?' hissed a gruff voice. "Get out. No one's allowed in 'ere, specially kids."

Not stopping to find out who he was, I scrambled for the exit then hobbled back through the throngs in the corridor to the sanctuary of the third-class carriage, where Gran was enjoying 40 winks. Shaking, I quietly slipped into my seat and for the remainder of the journey sat close to my gran, looking at a comic.

By the time the train pulled into the buffers at Southampton station, I could see through the window a busy quayside littered with luggage and hundreds of people. Bands playing, streamers flying, a buzz of excitement filled the air. Gran had one of her heads coming on. Swooning for a second, she grasped my shoulder to steady herself.

Running into the P&O ticket office, I immediately saw my younger sister looking yucky (my word for sickly sweet): new pink frilly frock, black patent shoes with straps and a big pink bow on her shiny brown head. My sibling had her own large travel trunk with her name printed on it and a big red sticker slapped on one side which read *TRIPOLI.*

"It's Tripoli, Jacqueline. In Libya. Africa." Gran sounded agitated. I now knew my sister was not boarding a boat just to hop over to the Isle of Wight.

"Which boat are they going on?" I said to Gran, looking up.

"That one. And it's a ship not a boat." Well, whatever it was, it was big—and I mean big. The only boat I had been on was one of those pleasure things along Southend seafront. I'd been on a rowing boat a few times on a boating lake but didn't suppose that counted. Mum had promised to take me on the Royal Daffodil one day.

At that moment, a rather pompous lady in a giant floppy hat floated by followed by a small porter, staggering under the weight of the lady's excessive luggage. Her commanding voice drifted across.

"Now then young man. Are you absolutely sure you have them all?"

I counted eight of all shapes and sizes. Surely that was all. Suddenly, the hatbox lid flipped open and out popped a furry creature. A magician couldn't have conjured it better.

Floppy Hat shrieked.

"Oh, my little Fifi!"

Little Fifi shot off like a bullet along the quay, chased by two little girls. Dragging my sister up the narrow gangway, I ran in hot pursuit. As soon as we reached the top, I caught sight of the little dog's white fluffy tail before it disappeared round a corner. Dodging hordes of excited passengers, we followed down the steps to B deck, swerving to avoid a huddle of people and bumping into a waiter, sending him and his full tray of drinks hurtling backwards.

Catching up, we finally cornered Fifi. Grabbing and cuddling the little animal, we made our way back down the gangplank on to the quay, where Floppy Hat showed her gratitude by pressing a coin into each of our small hands.

My eyes sparkled. Hot in my palm was a whole shiny sixpenny piece, the largest coin I had ever possessed. Rushing back to show Gran, I was intercepted by a screaming Aunt Peggy.

"Look what you've done," she screeched, "you horrible, horrible girl."

She was pointing at Susan, skirt now a dirty pink, scuffed patent shoes, pretty ribbon missing. My aunt lunged at me. I tried to dodge her but was grabbed by my bunches and swung around. Then I felt the sting on my face. Holding my cheek I began to cry, gripping the sixpence tightly in my hand.

"You can cry all you like. It won't get you anywhere," hissed my aunt forcefully.

Soon it was time to leave, time to exchange goodbyes. I had to kiss the aunt and uncle who were taking my sister away. His moustache tickled; hers itched.

For a fleeting moment I wondered why my little playmate was leaving me. But I was getting used to people going. A few months earlier, my other sister, younger than Susan and me, wasn't in her cot one morning. No one talked about it. No one explained. Adults don't, do they?

I stood close to our grandmother on the dock, with all the other relatives and friends, as my sister was hustled up the gangway by my aunt, followed gingerly by my uncle. I didn't mind my aunt and uncle leaving. In fact, I was pleased she was going. But I didn't want my sister to leave.

Sirens and trumpets blasted, people waved and shouted, coloured confetti cascaded down, blanketing the quayside. With an aching arm, I frantically waved my little Union Jack, searching the sea of faces along the ship's rail.

Susan was nowhere to be seen, but Gran said she could see her.

Chapter 4
Going to School on an Egg

"Don't know what to do with you, child. You're so wilful," Gran would say to me. I was never sure whether this was meant as a compliment. No one explained. Adults often seemed to say things that children didn't understand.

Back at Gran's flat, scripture readings resumed at breakfast time and prayers before sleep at night. The latter routine has followed me through my life.

"She's a proper tomboy," I overheard Gran say one day, "too boisterous by far. It's the only way."

So, early one bright sunny September morning after breakfast, which of course included a boiled egg from my chickens (I never knew which one), Gran announced:

"I'm taking you somewhere today, Jacqueline." I knew straightaway this was something different. She only said my full name if cross or uncertain, and she wasn't cross.

"Where to, Gran?" I asked with excitement.

"Away for a sort of holiday, you know."

The trouble was I did not know.

The brown suitcase had already been packed with a few clothes: Two white liberty bodices, two pairs of navy knickers, one pleated skirt, two blouses, one cardigan, two pairs of socks, nightclothes. Not many personal things. One favourite toy.

Before leaving for this holiday, I ran to the bottom of the garden, having one important task to perform. "Bye Emily. Bye Sarah. Be good girls. Don't be too noisy or they'll get rid of you too."

Poking my small, thin fingers through the wire netting, I tossed my two pet chickens a handful of corn and accepted their clucking as gratitude.

Emily, the elder of the pair, was a little on the large size but a good-natured bird. It would take a lot to ruffle her dark brown feathers—unless downwind of a certain marauding fox that stalked the neighbourhood. Though much smaller, Sarah made up for it by flapping and fussing more often than necessary. She shadowed Emily everywhere, usually so close that her beak almost touched Emily's parson's nose.

Some children took dogs and even cats on leads for walks. I took chickens.

Gran had made special harnesses from old pieces of material. She was clever like that. Emily's was pink, Sarah's blue, their names embroidered on the front.

"We must look after them," Gran always clucked.

She was right. I went to school on an egg. Other children went on the bus.

Just outside the back door stood the small brick outhouse where the chickens lived, with shelves on whitewashed walls and several trays for storage. Both chickens seemed to respond to my pampering, becoming champion layers. Honestly, you would think there were hundreds of hens not just two. Gran insisted it was due to her special feed mix and the good Lord, of course. "Our eggs will only have brown shells as they have more goodness in them," prophesied Gran. I never did find out what went into the 'special' mix, but I told her it was because they knew we loved them. Gran just laughed.

Surplus eggs were sold to friends and neighbours. Three times a week, I would be entrusted with a wicker shopping basket.

"Here's the latest batch, and don't break any!"

On one such occasion, I climbed the metal stairs at the back of the flats with my precious cargo then accidentally dropped a box over the side. It crashed into a tree, broken eggs slowly trickling down on to Mrs Kemp's washing.

I didn't go to school on an egg for a whole week.

People had grown used to seeing me strutting up and down the paved walk through in front of the flats. One horrible boy, older than me, always rode by on his bike shouting "Sage and onion!". I insisted their names were Emily and Sarah.

Gran lived at number 4, Mr and Mrs Kemp next door at number 5, another ground-floor flat like Gran's but on the end of the row. Now and then Mrs Kemp would invite Gran in for afternoon tea. There was always a lecture beforehand.

"You must behave yourself. She's not used to children." The Kemps never did have any, but they did have a dog, a corgi like the Queen, named Billy.

Afternoon tea was a grand occasion. Gran wore her best frock, freshly washed and pressed, her permed grey hair shining after a blue rinse; me a clean dress and white ankle socks with polished shoes.

Tea was served in posh looking cups with gold rims and saucers to match. Not like ours. No cracks or chips. A table was set with a starched white embroidered tablecloth and napkins. You could see Gran loved it. Her little finger would cock up as she held her teacup. A freshly baked strawberry jam sponge cake stood centre stage on a white doily atop a fancy silver cake stand. Constantly plumping cushions, our hostess hovered around me checking that no crumbs were being dropped on to her recently vacuumed carpet. Billy loitered nearby in case they were.

If Billy slipped from the house, and he often would as he was a clever little dog, particularly when the postman came, he would shoot out of the gate as quick as lightning. Mrs Kemp would become frantic. A search party would immediately form, hunting the area until the little dog was found, usually down at Old Mother Selby's place. She had a parrot chained to a perch in the front garden which spent most of his time calling out obscenities to passersby. "Put your hands over your ears," I was told. "That bird has a foul mouth." It took Gran some time to realise it was not Mr Selby working in the front garden who kept calling out "Give us a kiss!" every time we went by.

One day we set off, a bus ride down to Brentwood station. Another train, another journey to London, the second time in so many months. Some might say I was becoming a seasoned traveller. It was a habit I could easily get used to. Travelling on trains was exhilarating: the smell of the smoke, corridors filled with people, porters pushing large barrows stacked high with trunks and cases. We didn't need a porter, my suitcase being tatty and insignificantly small. As ever, Gran carried a bag which contained her *Women's*

Own magazine. I had an old *Beano*. I couldn't read the big words but loved the pictures. After navigating the underground, which still fascinates me, we reached our destination: Penge.

I followed Gran over the green wooden bridge spanning the railway line, dragging my feet. We walked in silence. A short distance from the station, Gran suddenly stopped outside an enormous brick building set behind a low stone wall mounted by tall iron railings. I peered through. Nothing but concrete with a tree here and there.

"Well, here it is," said Gran as though something important had been found. Squeezing her hand, I trudged after her up the steps to a large wooden front door. Gran lifted the big brass knocker.

"What's this place, Gran?"

"This is where you will be staying for a short while."

Why don't grown-ups tell you what's going on? Or at least give some sort of warning so you can get used to the idea. On this occasion, as on so many others, I was told nothing.

I was stepping back, clutching my toy—a stuffed rabbit—when a lady with a kind face opened a window.

"You new here then?"

And, before Gran could answer,

"Round the back."

Round the back was a kitchen where the lady, dressed in white, met us. Short and stout, she looked like an angel.

"Matron's not here at the moment. I'm Sister, and I'm in charge of sickbay.

"Now then," she paused, looking at me inquisitively, her nose twitching like a rabbit. I began to feel like a shrunken Alice after drinking the magic liquid.

Sister peered at me through gold-rimmed spectacles perched on the end of her nose.

"Who have we here then?"

Before I could speak, my grandmother answered. "This is Jacqueline."

"Ah yes," added Sister in Charge of Sickbay looking pleased, as though she had just solved some great mystery.

"Been expecting you. Come with me. Say goodbye dear."

It all happened so quickly. One minute Gran was there, the next gone. Sister held my suitcase in one hand and took my wrist in the other. We ascended a long, straight flight of stairs. In the distance shone a bright light. Was this the stairway to heaven that Gran spoke about. Was He up there?

I felt empty. I wanted Gran. At the top a square-galleried landing opened out with many coloured doors leading off it.

Sister led me into a large, white-walled room with a high ceiling and square bay windows. Eight high metal beds stood to attention, evenly spaced, each covered with a green and white counterpane.

"Here you are. Tell me, dear, does your grandmother call you Jacqueline or Jackie?"

"Jackie." My voice sounded soft and small.

"Well, Jackie, you take the second bed on the left. Unpack your things and then come downstairs. The bathroom's along the landing. Blue door. All right?"

I had lost my voice so just nodded.

No, it's not all right. I want to go home.

Suddenly she was gone. I was alone. Where were the others? Gran promised there would be other children.

My suitcase lay in the centre of the second bed on the left, though normally this wasn't allowed. A special privilege for the new girl.

Unsnapping the fasteners (no key needed, Gran said, as there was nothing of value to lock away) I lifted out the few things that had accompanied me and placed them in a white painted bedside locker.

I piled my liberty bodices, socks and knickers into it. A Gran-made dressing gown, red slippers, two hand-knitted cardigans and skirts for weekends followed. School uniform would be provided. If anything else was needed, Gran would post it to me.

At the bottom of the suitcase I found it. Sniffing hard, I lifted out the *King James Bible,* which Gran insisted I read every day, and a picture book of *The Snow Goose,* a present from Auntie Myrtle, Gran's daughter-in-law, the one I liked who lived in the country and made yummy scones.

A short time later Sister swiftly ushered me into a brightly lit room with the word *Matron* on the door, which quickly closed behind me. Standing in front of a large wooden desk, I was commanded to "Sit down girl" by an austere voice.

I presumed she meant me. There was no one else around. I perched on a hard wooden high-backed chair, inches from the desk. Matron put on her spectacles, which hung from a red cord around her neck. "So, what's your name, girl?" The commanding voice continued. My mind blank, I opened a dry mouth to speak but no words came out. Matron tutted. "Cat got your tongue?"

I don't remember seeing a cat, and I could still feel my tongue.

"Well, how old are you?"

"Six, Miss," I whispered.

"Quite so. Tall for your age, are we not?"

Matron only said that because she was short.

The woman looked down, shuffling papers. Quickly looking up, peering over the top of her specs, she said, "I see you suffer from loquacity?"

Do I? I feel all right. I don't remember being ill but didn't wish to appear ignorant.

"No, Miss. I mean yes, Miss."

Which was the right answer? I had no idea.

"I see," Matron said, drumming her fingers on the desktop. I was glad she did because I certainly did not. The interview was soon over, her exit as swift as my entrance.

What seemed like hours later, the kitchen door burst open and several children poured in. They were all dressed alike: boys in grey trousers and jumpers, white shirts, grey blazers and caps with green badges; girls wearing green and white striped dresses, straw hats with green and white bands of ribbon and the same blazers as the boys.

My loneliness dissipated. I thought how posh they all looked and couldn't wait to wear my uniform. Sitting at the kitchen table, I was mesmerised, with pictures ferrying around my brain. I saw myself older, parading up and down a catwalk wearing the latest Norman Hartnell creation.

That's what I want to be, I thought—a mannequin.

Chapter 5
The Little Heroine

The Easter holidays arrived. Sitting alone on my bed, sandwiched between white, heavily starched sheets, I was spending them isolated in sickbay. I heard the buzz of the other children excitedly packing suitcases to journey home and wondered why I wasn't with them.

My tattered brown suitcase stood beside my bed.

"I'm afraid," said Sister Teresa, ruefully, "you're not well enough to travel. You have a temperature."

Of course I have a temperature. What's she talking about? Without one I would be dead. That much I had learned at school.

Was it high or low? What number? No one said. But I did feel different. My arms and legs were itchy and stinging, so Sister painted me from head to foot in some smelly pink liquid.

"This will stop the irritation," she said, nose twitching, glasses at half mast as usual.

Her smile made me feel warm and happy.

A morgue would have had more life in it than sickbay though. There was only Sister to keep me company. And she spent most of her time in the office.

Strains of *Swan Lake* echoed along the white painted corridor. I pushed my feet into red slippers, ballet shoes in my imagination, and tied the red satin ribbons. Arms outstretched and standing on tiptoe, I pirouetted around the polished wooden floor. A pink nightie was my tutu.

The stage was set. The conductor tapped his baton, the orchestra was ready. I began to tread the boards, weaving in and out of empty beds, twirling round and round, spinning and gliding. As the music faded, I sank to the floor. The audience went wild with appreciation, throwing flowers at my feet. Markova!

I looked down at my feet. Yes, the red slippers were covered in flowers all right but they were also soaking wet. Oh no! One twirl too many had sent a vase of daffodils plummeting. Sister suddenly appeared carrying a mop and bucket, steaming carbolic, and silently mopped up the mess.

"I think it best you get back into bed," she suggested in her comforting lilt. Tucking me in, she said, "Do you like jelly and ice cream, Jackie?"

Did I like ice cream? If I were rich and lived in one of those big houses up on Eastbury Park, I would eat ice cream every day.

I just nodded and grinned as she made her exit, singing. She didn't even tell me off.

Some while later, wondering where my ice cream had got to, I slithered out of bed, my legs too short to reach the floor, and tiptoed to the ward door, pushing it gently and sidling through.

Along the white-walled corridor could be heard the sound of raised voices coming from the dispensary. Hearing cupboard doors being banged, I slipped silently into the sickbay office next to the dispensary. Not wishing to be seen, I crouched down behind the desk. Good. No sign of anyone. I noticed a light on in the dispensary and two dark figures silhouetted through the opaque glazing.

On the office desk stood Sister's wireless. I turned the knob but no sound came out. I knew I would be reprimanded for being out of bed, especially without slippers on, and daring to enter the office without permission, but was willing to take the risk.

On turning the second knob, with a sudden click the wireless burst into life. The sounds next door ceased but something was happening. The doorknob turned. After peering round the office door, two masked figures rushed from the dispensary along the corridor towards the exit.

I found Sister sitting on the floor, hands and feet tied with bandages. I pulled the plaster gag off, and she gulped the air. "Quick, help get these off," she said, and I undid the bandages. Once free, she staggered to the office and grabbed the telephone to dial 999. In a faltering voice, she said, "This is Sister Teresa at the school in Roding Close. We've been burgled."

I was agog and shivering, having forgotten to put my dressing gown on.

"Jackie, you did splendidly." I wondered what I had done.

"Can I have my ice cream now?"

"Of course. You can have two bowls if you wish."

The scream of the siren grew louder and stopped when the car it belonged to stood in front of the building. Two policemen accompanied Sister to the dispensary while I sat in the office chair, eating my reward. Suddenly the door opened. Sister entered, followed by the two policemen.

"These gentlemen want to talk to you, Jackie."

"Now then," said the older one with warm brown eyes and a soft smile. "We understand you saw the robbers."

I told them I saw two people running down the corridor.

"What were they wearing?" asked the second man, who was younger, with blue eyes and brown hair.

"They had masks on."

I tried to help with their enquiries as best I could, but it had all happened so quickly. Sister Teresa had already told them everything.

It was two o'clock the following afternoon (I knew because the little hand was on the two and the big hand on the 12). Kathleen Tabor, my grandmother, strutted through the swing doors, carefully carrying a small cardboard box.

My pulse raced. No one had mentioned that she was coming. She dared to sit on the bed, on the pristine counterpane, and hug her eldest grandchild tightly. Maybe she wasn't well. It was totally out of character. But it was good to smell her lavender water again. I felt that this was the one person in the whole world who loved me. Years later I would learn the truth.

"I hear you are quite the little heroine."

"Well, I…"

"Why, child, you only scared off a drug raid," she cooed.

"A what, Gran?"

"Those two horrible masked bandits were going to take pills from the medicine room. Anyway Jackie, how are you today? Pity the pox getting you like that."

"What, Gran?" I still hadn't been told what was wrong with me.

"Don't you know? It's chickenpox you've got. Chickenpox. As she stood up, from the rear view she looked like someone astride a horse, wearing a brown jacket which flared out over her backside.

"And talking of chickens…"

She handed me the small box. Itching to know what it contained, I untied the yellow ribbon. Inside were two eggs of identical size, one painted red, the other blue.

"Easter eggs from the girls," Gran proudly announced. I could never tell the difference between the eggs, whose was whose. They always looked alike to me, brown and oval. But Gran, bless her, reckoned she knew. She kept a sort of diary, showing how many they'd laid. The numbers always came out even.

Today the most important question had been answered: Emily and Sarah were still strutting strong.

"What happened to your lovely long hair?"

Of course she noticed. How could she not? Looking at her disapproving expression, I burst into tears. "They cut it off."

"There, there. Don't take on so." She gently stroked my short bob. "It'll soon grow again. You'll see. When you're older, you can wear it what length you like."

Opening her old brown handbag, she rummaged around and pulled out a lavender-scented handkerchief, dabbing my spotty forehead.

"Smells lovely, Gran." Sniffing it, I noticed the monogram in the corner: *K*. Kitty often did needlework. She had clever fingers.

"Does it? Well you keep it."

I felt as though she had given me the crown jewels. Grandmother never—never—gave presents, even for birthdays and especially at Christmas on account of her religious beliefs. She always said: "You don't need presents at set times of the year. I'll buy you something as and when you need it." And that was that with Gran. Her hankie would stay with me for many years to come.

"Oh, here's another present for you. Nearly forgot." Delving into her shopping bag, ever the hoarder ("it will come in handy one day"), Gran searched through the things she always carried no matter what—ration books, old bus tickets, cotton reels—until she eventually retrieved a creased brown-paper parcel tied up with string.

"It's from Mr Kemp.

From Mr Kemp? (Round red face, dark moustache, wavy dark hair.) What would Mr Kemp be sending me?

"He made it himself, you know. Well, open it then," urged Gran.

As I tore the wrapping off, Gran seemed as excited as me.

A brand new satchel, not second-hand, not hand-me-down but brand new. I could smell the leather and, lifting the flap, saw my full name printed inside. Also there was a wooden pencil case full of sharpened pencils with my initials on the lid.

"Isn't he clever?"

Gran explained that Mr Kemp had thought the episode with the eggs dripping on to his wife's washing the funniest thing he had ever seen and hadn't stopped cackling for days. It was the first time, he told Gran, that Mrs Kemp had been lost for words.

"Why don't you write him a thank-you letter?" suggested Gran.

"But what about your train, Gran?"

She checked her watch, always carried in her handbag. "Plenty of time. Another hour yet."

With a sheet of paper and a new pencil, I began.

"You're right-handed, aren't you?"

"Yes Gran." I wondered why she needed to confirm that.

"Good because when your mother was about your age we found her to be left handed. And in those days it was considered a bad thing."

My eyes were wide. "What you mean, Gran?" Now she had me hooked.

"Well, people looked upon left handers as sort of, well, different. Some said they were evil, witches even."

"Did they want to burn them at the stake?"

"No dear, not quite that bad," said Gran, horrified. "Anyway, she had to stay behind after school every day for half an hour to practise writing with her right hand."

"And did she?"

"Oh, yes. In fact, she became so good that the next term she won a handwriting competition," Gran glowed with pride.

"It's good I'm not left handed," I said as pictures flashed through my head of people being herded towards huge bonfires, right handers jeering and holding placards saying *Down with Left Handers.*

"Oh, it doesn't matter today. Being left handed is no longer considered a handicap. In fact, some folks reckons it shows you have brains."

I thought I knew what she meant.

As I began the letter, Gran rattled on about the neighbours in Western Gardens. "Number 1 have moved out. Gone to Australia on the government £10 voucher, they have. Don't know when new people will move in. Old Mrs Harvey at number 7 passed away a fortnight ago this Friday. She's been ill for years, and they didn't find her until two days later. Number 8 had burglars last month. Dunno why they bothered. Shouldn't think there was much in there worth taking. And she's walked out on him again at number 10. Good riddance to bad rubbish I say. Now then, next door, number 2, she's gone on a long holiday—to Spain of all places. Costa something or other. I reckon it cost her a packet. Still, some peoples have all the luck. Oh, and Billy's not been too well. Like you really."

"Billy's ill, Gran?" Now she had my full attention. "What's wrong with him?"

"Dunno really, but the vet gave him an injection."

I shivered. "Poor Billy. I bet he didn't like that. I hate them."

"Not quite the same, Jackie. Billy is a dog"

"Course he is, but he still has feelings." Gran looked surprised.

"Yes child. So much wisdom from one so young. You know, I think he's missing you."

"Just like Mum missing Dad," I blurted. Whoops.

"Of course not," snapped Gran. "Nothing like it." I knew I had dared to mention the unmentionable.

My head down, I finished the letter, which Gran folded and deposited in her handbag—probably to be lost forever.

Too soon it was time. Gran strutted out of the door, no hug this time, and I felt isolated again.

By the time my spots had disappeared, and my temperature hovered at a healthy 98.6 degrees, the

Easter holidays, and my isolation, were over. I was no longer lonely. Another term began.

Chapter 6
Crocodile Line

Thursdays were spelling test days. I hated Thursdays but not today. Today I was looking forward to going to school and the usually dreaded test. Determined to do well, I had spent much spare time learning all the words and was confident of getting full marks. 20 out of 20 and a gold star if lucky.

Now the start of the summer term, porridge was no longer on the breakfast menu—just when I was getting used to it, lumps and all. Today I would tuck into soggy cornflakes, followed by an overdone piece of toast, heaped, if I could get away with it, with orange marmalade, decorating the edge of my plate with the bits.

Going to school each morning was a highly military operation. Children walked in twos in a straight line behind each other. Being the last, and an odd number, I often followed at the end of the crocodile, usually on my own. This particular morning was bright and sunny. We marched past semi-detached houses exhibiting colourful flowers and shrubs in neat front gardens. Birds twittered in green treetops swaying in the gentle breeze. My new, freshly starched (everything seemed to be starched) summer uniform, especially the cream boater banded with a green ribbon, gave me a feeling of belonging. With my new satchel slung over my shoulder, I strode along, softly singing to myself.

Had a good home when he left
Serves him jolly well right

It was a little ditty Gran and I often sang, walking in step, left right, left right up the High Street back home in Brentwood.

Suddenly someone grabbed my arm and pulled me into the bushes. About to cry out, I saw my mother smiling down at me. "Mum, what…?"

"Shh, it's all right. Haven't seen you for ages. Thought we'd have a day out together," she whispered.

It was quite true. The last time we had seen one another was during the Christmas holidays, when I stayed with Gran at her flat for a few weeks. That was a whole half-year ago.

Perhaps not seeing her eldest daughter at Easter had made my mother more unsettled. Poor Mum. She only had me left now. The other two had gone. (I still did not know where my youngest sister went.) By sending me away, they thought it would cure Mum. Of course, it had the adverse effect.

"I've got to go to school," I protested, thinking of the full marks and three house points.

"Don't you want to come?"

"Not today, Mum. Today I've got spelling and I know them all," I boasted.

"That's gratitude for you. I've come all this way."

I stood looking down at my new brown sandals.

"What about my uniform? I'll get into trouble if I mess it up."

"I've thought of that Jackie." She patted a red holdall. "Here are your old clothes. You can change at the station."

"Where we going?" The idea was beginning to grow on me.

"How about the seaside?"

Now she was talking.

"Southend?"

"If you like."

Emerging from the bushes, I peered down the road. The crocodile line had disappeared round the corner. It was probably halfway to school by now. We walked the short distance to the railway station, and Mum bought tickets at the ticket office then helped me change in the ladies' waiting room. Mum had a cup of tea. Then the train came and we were on our way. I took the brown paper bag Mum handed me. Aniseed balls. She'd remembered.

"Ta Mum. Haven't had these for ages."

On the journey, Mum told me it was her day off from the hospital. I watched out of the window—cows in the fields, tractors ploughing—remembering the happy times I had spent with my dad and sister when we lived in the countryside.

A few hours later the train pulled up against the buffers at Southend Victoria.

"I'm thirsty, Mum."

"So am I. We'll pop into Garon's." A popular tea shop not far from the railway station, Garon's was a good, regular watering hole for tourists and locals, who would stop for hot drinks and sometimes a bun.

Further down the High Street, I followed my mother, who seemed to be on a mission, into Keddies, a large department store. Riding the lift was my favourite thing about Keddies. After a while of trawling around looking at everything but buying nothing, Mum announced that it was my turn to choose.

I knew exactly where I wanted to go. With that we headed down towards Pier Hill, down the steps and across the road to Peter Pan's Playground. The famous mile-and-a-quarter pier stretched like a long tentacle into the glistening sea. I loved this place.

"You can choose three rides," Mum said, peering into her purse. No problem there. My first choice was the Animal Train. Sitting high up front on a charging elephant, I was now on safari in Africa, thundering across the plains, chasing tigers and rhinos. I wondered if my sister Susan did this in Libya. After all, Libya is in Africa. I learned that at school. Zigzagging around the narrow track in circles, waving to Mum sitting on a bench nearby, I thought how lovely she looked with the sun shining on her dark hair piled on top of her head and pretty floral dress. Today was obviously a good one.

My second choice was the helter-skelter. A long climb to the top was followed by a swift whizz down on a rush mat, screaming, as everybody did, at the top of my voice, the ride over far too soon.

Now for my final choice. The big wheel or the Crooked House? I chose the Crooked House with its funny shaped chimney. It was difficult to stand up and walk along rickety floorboards, as if there was some great force of gravity pulling me back.

Once the tickets were used up, I told Mum I was hungry. "Must be the sea air," she reasoned.

"What do you fancy?"

The inviting aroma of fish and chips wafted across the seafront, making the decision for us.

The sun kissed the two happy day trippers sitting near the beach, munching a much welcomed lunch out of newspaper—the only way to eat it.

When a gypsy stopped by to read Mum's palm, I kicked off my socks and shoes and ran down to the water's edge, tucking my dress into my navy knickers. The tide was in, the air salty. Pieces of seaweed floated on the water's edge, the sulphurous smell tickling my nostrils. Seagulls hovered overhead, swooping down, scavenging scraps of the food that littered the sand and the shoreline.

I giggled at the sensation of mud squelching between my toes. That was the trouble with Southend: mud stretched hundreds of yards out into the estuary, a huge black expanse—a haven for bait diggers but not today. Today people packed the shore, revelling in the high tide, not giving a thought as to what lay beneath the muddy yet still shimmering water. Gran insisted mud was good for you, especially when ill. She had lots of sayings on account of her Victorian grandmother.

Not knowing how long I had paddled, nor how far along the beach I had wandered, when I turned around Mum was nowhere to be seen. Frantically searching the crowded beach, weaving in and out of day trippers in deckchairs, men with hankies on heads tied in all four corners, picnic baskets, sandcastles, buckets and spades, I could still see no sign of her. Feeling frightened, I began to cry as it dawned on me that I was lost.

Soon a kindly voice spoke to me. "Now, what's the matter dear?"

Wiping my eyes on my arm, I looked up to see a police lady.

I sobbed. "I can't find my mum."

"Never mind," the soft voice continued. "I'll help you find her."

She asked my name and age and held my small hand as we walked along the promenade. Some while later we arrived at the police station.

"Who you got there then, Marge?" asked a friendly man behind the desk.

"It's Jackie, and she's lost her mum," replied Marge, giving my hand a squeeze.

"Hello Jackie. I'm Bill. Now, you come and sit round here. I think I've got some Huntley & Palmers somewhere," he said, rummaging in the desk drawer.

The big clock on the police station wall said three o'clock. Bill was kept busy seeing to people coming in and answering the telephone. Dozing in the big chair, I suddenly awoke, feeling a hot sensation on my leg. Looking down, I saw a bedraggled black and white dog panting and wagging its tail.

"Someone to keep you company," laughed Bill. "He's lost too, and he's been in the sea."

The dog shook himself dry, and I welcomed the spots of water despite the doggy smell. They felt cool and refreshing in the hot, stuffy police station. The dog finally laid down at my feet, and I fed my last biscuit to him. Two lost souls together.

Later, a young boy ran into the police station. "You got a dog in here, mister?" he enquired. At the sound of his master's voice, the damp, scruffy dog quickly jumped up, rushing towards the boy, bouncing up and down and nearly knocking him off his feet. Dog and owner reunited.

"Wish that was me going home," I said with a sigh. Some time later the station door flew open and an agitated person spilled in looking hot and bothered. I was relieved to see a familiar face.

"Oh, there you are," said Gran. "Been worried out of my wits." She hugged me as my mother appeared in the doorway, accompanied by a policeman.

"Why did you do that?" exploded Gran.

"I only…" I started.

"Not you," said Gran, "your mother."

"I just wanted to see her," Mum said lamely.

I ran to her, burying my small face in her skirt. "I couldn't find you."

"Sorry love, had to spend a penny. When I got back you were gone."

"Well, never mind that. She's safe now." Gran sounded very cross.

Then, turning to Mum, she said, "Do you realise what you have done? The authorities think she's been abducted." Now that sounded painful.

The policeman ushered us into a small room and began firing questions at me.

"When did your mother meet you? Where did she meet you?"

"How did you get to Southend?"

I told him. "Mum isn't a witch," I added. She's not left handed any more cause she can now write with her right hand."

The sergeant scratched his balding head and mopped his sweating brow.

"Now look here young lady…"

"I think she's had too much sun," interrupted Gran, quickly hustling me towards the door and the waiting police car.

"Where we going, Gran?"

"Back to school young lady."

Wriggling free from her iron grip, I ran back to Mum, who put a protective arm around me.

Not a word spoken, Gran pulled me away.

"But what about Mum?"

"Oh, she'll be all right. They'll just tell her off."

That's funny, I thought, Mum getting told off instead of me.

Chapter 7
Who Dares

Once back at school, I quickly realised I had become something of a celebrity. I didn't really understand what all the fuss was about. The following day the local newspaper even carried a short account of the 'abduction' and concluded by stating: *She was found safe and well and returned to the bosom of her family.*

Suddenly the other boys and girls wanted to be my friend and my sweet ration increased. Three children who became close to me, or as close as any human can become to another in these circumstances, were Brian, nearly seven, and twins Maureen and George, six and three quarters. They were all older than me at six and five months.

Moving around to different addresses as often as I did, not staying in one place for long, made it difficult, if not nearly impossible, to make firm friends with other children.

As soon as I became used to them and them to me, I would be whisked off to pastures new and strange people. But now back at school, I had the whole of the rest of the term to make friends with my fellow inmates.

Brian, brown straight hair parted in the middle, large brown eyes and long lashes, liked his food, and it more than showed. If it was sweets or biscuits he desired, Brian would find a way to get them from somewhere or other. A born organiser, Brian was the natural leader of our 'gang'.

Although twins, Maureen and George did not resemble one another at all. In fact, they did not even look as if they were related. Often they had to insist they were twins after being accused of telling fibs. Maureen was a tubby, dark-brown-haired, dark-eyed girl, while her brother, ten minutes older, was wiry, ginger-haired and blue eyed. The four of us were an odd assortment.

Brian, bolder than any of us, particularly enjoyed playing dares. It became our favourite game.

At night, after lights out, we would dare each other to do certain things, not really bad things you understand, just enough to get a good telling off.

The most popular dare soon became gathering biscuits for a midnight feast. Of course, this was Brian's idea.

We would take it in turns to tiptoe, shoeless, down the wide staircase, through the large hallway, along a narrow corridor into forbidden territory—the kitchen. No child, under any circumstances, was allowed in the kitchen. The pantry door was kept locked during daytime when children were about. At nighttime it was left unlocked.

So, when we were supposed to be tucked up in bed, we discovered that it was easy to gain access to whatever we wanted. There was only one problem we encountered: bumping into members of staff. They were usually off duty but still up and about after lights out. Luckily, we found many places small children could hide undetected.

We four friends played this dare many times, and only once did someone get caught—or came close to it.

It was a Friday night and Maureen's turn.

"I don't want to do it," she moaned.

"But it's your turn, and you know the rules," pressured Brian.

"I don't want to. I feel sick."

George, the ever protective sibling, looked with concern at his sister.

"I'll do her turn if you like," he said.

So George stood in for Maureen. It was on his way there that the obstacle appeared: he ran into Sister.

"I'm thirsty," he lied. Fortunately, she believed him as George was not the sort of boy who made a habit out of telling fibs or making a fuss. She ushered him into the kitchen, where she gave him a glass of water and promptly ordered him back to bed. To his relief, and ours, he had got away with it. But there was no midnight feast.

The biggest dare of all proved to be our undoing. It all started with George wanting some marbles.

"Well, let's go and get some," suggested Brian.

"We can't. No one's got any pocket money left," I chipped in.

"I've got sixpence," Maureen offered, checking her locker.

"Good," said Brian, "we'll go to the shops by bus."

"But what about the marbles?" asked George.

"We'll take them."

"You mean steal?"

"Yeah."

We looked at each other in amazement. I, for one, had never done anything like that. I might be classed as boisterous, but I wasn't naughty, not really naughty. It did sound like fun though.

"I'll come," I said on impulse.

"Me too," the twins echoed.

It was agreed. We would set off first thing after breakfast.

Saturday morning arrived. No one would miss us, not for hours anyway.

One thing we did not count on was a nit check. After breakfast, we all filed, one behind the other, into the dayroom, where Nurse stood at one end with a large nit comb.

This check was carried out periodically. Nurse would draw the large comb through our hair, one after another, leaving an awful-smelling substance on it. The ritual seemed to take ages, especially this particular morning.

Brian boasted that he had been into town a few times before, on his own of course, but had never told anyone. So he knew which bus to catch. He asked for four single halves to the Odeon, and the bus conductor clipped our tickets. When the double-decker bus dropped us off at the Odeon, we stepped into a tide of weekend shoppers and made a pact to stay together. No getting lost. (That is one thing I am good at.)

My eyes were drawn to the mesmeric, brightly coloured displays in the shop windows. It had been some while since I saw these sights.

"Let's go in here," suggested Brian, ducking into Woolworths with the rest of us in hot pursuit, not wishing to get separated.

I liked Woolies, as Mum called it. I could spend hours looking at all the different items for sale, all under a shilling, especially the vast array of brightly coloured sweets. It was while eyeing these delights that I suddenly saw Brian take a tube of sweets off the counter and pocket them. Too shocked to say anything, the twins and I silently but quickly followed him out of the store into the street.

"I saw you take those sweets," I confronted him.

"Fun, isn't it?" Brian laughed.

He stuffed them as fast as he could into his big mouth, not even offering them to us. No manners. I began wishing I had never ventured on this dare. By no means was I a Miss Goody Goody but I was no thief. Gran had taught me the Ten Commandments, and I knew stealing was wrong.

Putting a quick distance between us and Woolworths, we hurried behind Brian, further along the High Street, despite the crowds.

Not looking where he was going, Brian suddenly bumped into a robust lady wearing a huge hat, knocking her shopping bag out of her hand and scattering the contents on to the ground. Fruit and vegetables littered the pavement.

Grabbing Brian by the scruff of the neck, she roared like a lion.

"You careless boy. I ought to…" She never did finish that sentence.

"Why, Brian Hawkins. What are you doing here?" demanded the lady.

We looked up to see Matron's distorted, angry red face.

"Run you lot!" he shrieked, kicking Matron in the shins.

By now a small crowd had gathered to see what all the commotion was about.

Clutching Maureen's hand, I took off and darted into the shopping arcade, swerving in between shoppers with bags, dogs and prams, George hard on our heels. Rounding a corner, Maureen stopped abruptly. So did I.

"I've got a stitch," she panted, holding her side. Searching the sea of faces in the direction we had just come, we saw no sign of a ginger-haired boy, nor anyone else for that matter, in pursuit of us.

"We must get going, far away from here," I urged.

"Where to?" Maureen looked worried. "I'm really frightened."

"Me too. And I think we're lost."

I seemed to be making a habit of getting lost, but this was different. This time I knew that, if caught, we would be going back to school to face The Dragon.

If we could just find the Odeon, we could at least find the bus to take us back—as there was nowhere else to go. But there was one big snag: no money left for bus fares.

Wondering what to do, we decided to get out of the shopping arcade—and walked straight into the arms of the law.

"'ello, 'ello," said the policeman. "Been waiting for you two young ladies."

I could tell from Maureen's expression that she felt the same as me—pure, utter relief. A short while later, a police car drew up alongside the kerb.

"Look, the boys," I pointed out to Maureen, resignation sweeping over me. Brian looked mad, while George, surprisingly, appeared happy. By this time so were Maureen and I, and we were more than willing to squeeze in, though hungry and too tired to talk.

Back in school in Matron's office, the four of us, the worse for wear, stood in front of her desk.

"Well, what have you got to say for yourselves?"

In unison: "Sorry Miss."

"You do realise this little escapade will cost you dearly," Matron said, wagging her stubby finger in front of our scarlet faces. I could tell she was enjoying herself. "Firstly, you are all grounded for three weeks with no special privileges for the rest of the term."

None of us dared to look at the others, casting our eyes to the floor.

"Off you go," commanded Matron, waving us away with her hand. We filed out of the door, a pitiful looking quartet.

"Not you, Brian Hawkins," roared Matron. "I want a special word with you."

The door quickly slammed behind us three, leaving our leader inside to his fate with the irate dragon.

Brian never did tell us what Matron said behind the closed door, and no one else mentioned it either.

A few days later, excitement filled the air as preparations were made for a visit of some important people. Brian reckoned they were coming to see me on account of my being in the paper. But of course he got it wrong. The dignitaries were visiting Matron in honour of her retirement at the end of the summer term.

In the morning, tables were set and coloured bunting hung. Special cakes were baked, and after lunch everyone assembled in the school hall. Matron, wearing her best blue frock with white collar and red lipstick, sat sedately on the stage with other members of staff and the four officials. After speeches about what a lovely person she was (they should have asked us children) we sang a few songs. Then she was presented with a marble mantel clock for her long and valued service.

The last day of term soon arrived, with everyone excitedly packing suitcases and going home for the summer holidays. Matron packed hers for the last time. She was retiring to a Sussex cottage.

Due to further attempts made by my mother to 'abduct' me, each without success, and with the added episode of running away, I too was now packing my tattered old brown suitcase, never to return.

I had felt happy for a while with the companionship of our little gang. I never saw Brian and the twins again and often wondered what became of my partners in crime.

Chapter 8
Another Planet

Standing in front of a spotless glossy black door with a highly polished brass knocker and matching letterbox, my tatty brown suitcase at my feet, I waited with Gran. Finally, the door creaked open revealing a blue dress, white apron and mob cap. "Entre, entre. You have been expecting. Madame receive you in ze drawing room."

I looked up at Gran, who raised her eyes to heaven and shrugged her shoulders.

I followed my grandmother, who in turn followed Blue Dress, wondering what on earth Madame was drawing in the drawing room.

Perhaps my stay here wasn't going to be so bad after all. I liked drawing.

The drawing room, of good size, was not what I had expected. Several sofas dotted the room with brightly coloured cushions and gilt-edged paintings hanging from picture rails on pastel walls. At the end of the room stood a baby grand piano, the top of which was decorated with an assortment of china dolls, several painted vases and a selection of silver-framed sepia and black-and-white photographs of various people sporting happy expressions. At the other end of the drawing room was a chaise longue on which perched a smiling Madame.

Of small build and elegantly dressed, Madame's auburn hair was held high in an elaborate pleat. She wore make-up, lots of make-up, and her fingernails were long and painted.

I had never seen anyone like her. Well, only on the front cover of *Vogue,* the women's fashion magazine, which Mum read occasionally, when she could afford it.

Madame glided towards me, arms outstretched. "Mon petite Jacqueline."

This was unfamiliar territory. I tried to back away as Madame embraced me.

At that moment, a tall, slim, distinguished looking gentleman, sporting a small brown moustache, joined us.

"Please do sit down." He spoke perfect English and gestured towards a chair.

"I'm David. This is Marie, my wife, and Colette, our maid."

To everyone's surprise, Gran stood up. She had only just sat down.

"Well, I best be going," she said, nervously looking at the French clock on the mantel shelf.

"Be good for Mr and Mrs Clements." Planting a peck on my flushed cheek, she breezed from the room with Colette.

Sitting on the plush sofa, clutching my rabbit, I watched expectantly as the door slowly opened. Perhaps Gran had changed her mind and come back to get me. No. In waddled a black dog with a white patch on one ear.

"Ah Naige. Say 'ello to Jacqueline." I loved the way she pronounced my name. It sounded like singing. She led the dog across to where I sat, and he flopped his head on my small lap, waiting to be stroked, large dark eyes looking up at me. Naige and I became instant friends.

"He like you, cherie," said Madame. "Come now wiz Marie. I show you where you sleep."

Obediently following her up a short flight of steps to a small, but bigger, room than the one I used at Gran's flat, I felt the warmth and welcome envelop me as soon as she opened the door.

Pretty pink walls were covered with paintings of Bambi and other animals, floral curtains framed the window with a lampshade to match and the bed was swathed in the prettiest bed cover I had ever seen.

"You like?" enquired Marie, clasping her hands, eagerly awaiting my approval.

"Oh yes, I like. I mean, it's beautiful!"

"Bon! Très bon!"

Later I discovered from Colette—younger than Marie, brown hair, her English not as good as her employer's—that Madame had decorated the room herself, even painting the figures on the walls.

At dinner that evening, which was a grand affair compared to what I was used to, with a great choice of food, I learned that Marie came from Amiens, had met David Clements during the war and came back to England with him. Her famille still lived in France.

David was now a bank manager, and they lived in the large apartment above the bank where he worked. They had no children.

My life changed dramatically during the next few weeks. Marie had obviously been meticulously planning for my arrival for some time. I did wonder why I had not been told—yet again.

Bath time and bedtime had never been so fun. Marie poured scented, bubbly liquid into the water, which frothed up nearly to the bath's rim. That first night, before going to bed, Marie handed me a small red book.

"Zis, cherie, is for you. Sometimes I speak ze French, so I will teach you. You write in ze book so you learn ze French, non?"

So I wrote in the book: *non—no, oui—yes.*

"Bon! You learn two words already, oui?"

Smiling up at Marie, I mused that I had never seen such a pretty lady—nor one so kind. I had a feeling my stay would be a happy one.

Each night Marie would read a story to me, sometimes in English, other times in French. Though I didn't understand, I did recognise the pictures. Turning out the bedside lamp, edged with its pink frill, I thought of Gran and wondered if she still wrapped her nightdress over and around the lampshade to warm it before putting it on.

The following days were taken up with so many new and exciting experiences. It was like a waking dream.

Shopping became more interesting. As Naige was getting old in dog years, his back legs were weak, so when Marie shopped he rode on a small, wooden trolley raised a few inches above the ground with a little wheel at each of the four corners.

Marie often let me pull the trolley along into Woolworths and the ironmongers in Brentwood High Street, attracting an audience wherever we went. Marie and Naige were well known and well respected.

The morning of my eighth birthday was unforgettable. On my breakfast chair sat a parcel tied up with a large pink bow.

"Bon anniversaire!"

"Happy birthday!" David echoed.

My small fingers tore off the colourful wrapping and pulled out the most beautiful dress my young eyes had ever seen—pink with cream stripes and a small cream collar—and black patent shoes.

"Oh Marie, merci!" I flung my small arms around her neck, the aroma of perfume enfolding me. How could she know I wanted black patent shoes?

"A beautiful frock for a beautiful person. Try zem on. All ze best dressed girls are wearing zese." The shoes fitted perfectly.

"You wear zem when we go to London today."

"London? Today?"

"Oui, cherie. We go to see a show."

One hour later, David drove us to Brentwood station, and we were soon seated on the train, travelling first-class and steaming towards Liverpool Street.

Marie seemed to know her way around the underground, and before long we were lunching in a Lyons Corner House. From there we made our way to Her Majesty's Theatre, where the show *Brigadoon* was being staged.

"You see a show before?"

"Non." I was too excited to talk, watching in awe the alien sights, sounds and smells, the people, their clothes. So many different things. London truly was a magical place, just like Brigadoon. We sang 'Go Home With Bonnie Jean' all the way home.

Sometimes old Tom the gardener encouraged me to help him and let me explore his shed. He was a kindly man of middle age, with greying hair and a small moustache, thin weathered face and sparkling blue eyes. The garden behind the bank stretched for some 200 yards or so, with a small apple orchard at the bottom. Planting time kept Tom busy, putting in young vegetable seedlings. Madame liked everything fresh, Tom informed me. She insisted on healthy eating, with plenty of fresh fruit and vegetables. Tom grew them, Colette cooked them and we all ate them.

Marie also liked flowers. The garden and apartment were full of colourful, scented blooms with names I could never hope to remember, except the rose, which was Mum's favourite.

One sunny weekend, Marie announced we were all going to the seaside. Being a successful bank manager, David was the proud owner of a black Riley, his pride and joy, which he lovingly cleaned and polished every week. No one in my family had ever had a car, apart from Granddad for his business, and I didn't know of anyone who owned one. Aside from police cars, I had never really ridden in one.

"You like ze seaside?" Marie asked.

"I've been to Southend." I recalled the last time there with Mum.

"Today we go to Frinton. No get lost. We have a petite beach hut."

David played chauffeur, proudly taking the steering wheel of the gleaming Riley, soon packed inside and out with a large picnic hamper on the rear and its roof down. He looked so dashing in casual clothes and flat cap rather than the usual dark suit and tie. Marie sat beside him in a strapped lemon sundress and a large straw hat with coloured ribbons flowing from it, her clothes reflecting her happy mood. In the back sat Colette and me with Naige squashed between us.

Arriving at Frinton-on-Sea on the Essex east coast, I jumped out of the car and raced across the cliff top towards the sea. I was not prepared for the scene up ahead: ugly barbed wire fencing stretched across the beach, supported on large wooden struts.

"They should be taking those away soon," explained David. "It was put there in the war. Part of our coastal defence system." The information was completely lost on everyone. They were all too busy unpacking the car. Everyone loaded up, we traipsed down the cliff path to the promenade, where Marie suddenly stopped outside a freshly painted blue and white wooden hut the size of a small bungalow.

Spending the day on the beach, in the water, making sandcastles, jumping waves, exploring rock pools, collecting shells and pebbles, I was not sure who enjoyed it more—Marie, David, Colette or me. A truly magical day. Happiness warmed my bones.

Naige and I snoozed the whole way home.

Temperatures were high all day and didn't drop that night. Sleep was difficult, my window slightly open trying to catch a breeze. Later the storm started. I had experienced storms before but never like this one.

Marie heard my cries and was soon sitting on my bed, hugging and rocking me like a baby. Together we watched the lightning streak across the dark sky, thunder rumbling overhead. Naige trundled in and sat at the foot of the bed. He must be frightened too, I thought. As the storm began to subside, Marie explained, in soothing tones, that it was only the forces of nature coming together—whatever that meant. She stood in front of the partially opened window, inhaling the now fresher night air. Raising both her arms, she said, "Look at ze moon and stars. See how bright zey shine. We draw great energy from zese. Can you feel it, cherie?"

I wanted so much to feel this energy that I stood close to Marie, peering out into the blackness, watching the lightning fade into the distance, the only sound now the rain beating on the rooftop.

"Ma mère always say a storm is ze angels doing housework." Marie gently kissed my forehead and tucked me in bed. "Bon nuit, cherie."

Naige remained at the foot of my bed, as though his presence would protect me, and this became a nightly ritual. I cried softly to myself, as I had often done in the past, this time not because I was frightened but because of the warm feeling inside. I had never experienced this sensation before.

I wanted to stay here forever.

As the days spilled into weeks, I discovered a passion for something which Marie also loved—tennis. Belonging to a local club, Marie often took me with her. Having never held a racket, nor even seen a game of tennis, at first I found it awkward but with Marie's patience and guidance I soon learned how to hit the ball over the net and move my feet quickly to get into position for the next shot. This love of the sport stayed with me right up to senior school, when I would play for the school team.

One hot summer morning, Marie took me to Wimbledon to watch some of the great players of the day.

On the train journey (first-class again) Marie explained that men wore shorts, and the greatest woman player of all time was Suzanne Lenglen, a fellow Frenchwoman. 'La Divine', as she was known, won the championship when she was only

15 and went on to win five more Wimbledon finals. Louise Brough, the defending champion, would be this year's winner and would win again the following year.

One dismal rainy Saturday morning, the first rain for weeks, I sensed things were different. Something was happening. For one, Marie did not join me for breakfast but stayed in her room complaining of a headache—most unusual. In fact, I had never known her to suffer with one the entire time I had been staying with them. Also, David was nowhere to be seen.

When the doorbell sounded, Gran charged in. "Pack your case. You're coming home."

Tears welled up in my eyes. A feeling of nausea swept over me.

"No!" I shouted. "I want to stay. I love it here."

It was a red-eyed Colette who silently handed Gran my bulging tatty brown suitcase. They knew. They all knew. But no one had told me.

As Gran dragged me struggling out of the front door, there was still no sign of Marie. My last image was of Colette dabbing her eyes, standing on the doorstep with Naige. The old dog's ears and tail drooped sorrowfully.

I rode the bus in silence, apart from my sniffles. Neither of us spoke. I walked along the pathway in front of the familiar flats. Outside number 5 Mr

Kirby, cutting his hedge, commented, "Hi kid. Been quiet around here without you. Where you been?"

"Another planet, Mr Kirby," I mumbled softly. "Another planet."

My magical Brigadoon had evaporated in the mist of my tears.

Chapter 9
Flashback

Moon watching became a nightly ritual. When it was visible, especially during a storm, soaking up the moon's energy became my comforter. I felt sure Marie would also be gazing into the heavens. It made me feel close to her.

Some months earlier, when my father, mother, sister Susan and I were all living together as a 'normal' family in Domley Cottage in Great Leighs, my father, in one of his rages, ordered Mum to "Get out!". I was eavesdropping at the top of the stairs on the landing.

Thud! The door slammed and heavy bolts shot across like bullets. Rushing to my bedroom window, I caught a glimpse of Mum hurrying from the cottage.

Mummy. The familiar word sticking in my throat. Banging on the window pane. Lost in a clap of thunder.

Afraid. Leaping into bed. Hiding under the covers. Trying to stifle my crying.

Hiding from what? Could it be the storm, or perhaps my angry father? Mother locked out. Me locked in. He was downstairs. I was alone.

Desolation engulfed me. A short while later, hearing gentle tapping, I ventured out of bed, curiosity getting the better of me. I hurried back to the rain spat window. Standing on tiptoe, my small feet now accustomed to the cold, lino-covered floor, I peered through the gap in the faded floral curtains, straining my eyes into the darkness.

Peering down I could just make out mother's figure, stomach bulging under her clinging, wet dress, illuminated by a lightning flash. She sobbed and leant by the door, pleading.

"Ron, for God's sake let me in. I'm freezing."

With nose against the pane, I somehow felt that by staying by the window, watching, in my small way I could prevent something dreadful from happening.

Mum had not really been happy since moving to the farm. With Father as stubborn as he was, the arguments had become stronger and more violent during the past few months. I didn't really understand what the arguments were about, but they always ended up with Mum in tears. It had been that way for months, and we no longer saw Gran and Granddad.

It wasn't just the storm that night that I was trying to block out but the raised voices of my parents above the buffeting wind around the draughty farmhouse.

Eventually I heard the bolts shoot back and the door creak open.

"Shush Ron. Keep it down. You'll wake the girls."

Too late. I was already wide awake.

Mother's soft tone drifted upstairs, sending with it a moment of warmth and reassurance. I tried hard not to listen to their yelling, concentrating instead on the rain strumming against the attic window while I trembled beneath the bedcovers.

Tossing and turning, wanting to sleep but not daring to in case Mum needed me.

Moments later heavy footsteps sounded across the wooden hall floor. I automatically began counting: one, two, three, four, creak, six, seven. My heart raced. 12. 13. The metal latch echoed in the stillness. The bedroom door crashed against the wall. Father filled the doorway, wild with rage. I lay motionless, silently gulping shallow breaths as he strode towards me. Suddenly the bedclothes were flung back and he gripped my arm tightly. Seconds later I was yanked out of bed and hauled down the stairs, my feet hardly touching the ground. The stench of sweaty armpits and beery breath hot on my face made me swoon.

I was dropped in the middle of the sitting room floor. The shock of cold quarry tiles against my naked feet brought me quickly to my senses.

Hiding squinting eyes with trembling hands. Daring to peep through my small fingers.

Mother, quietly sobbing, stood crumpled beside the brick fireplace at one end of the room. My immediate instinct was to run to her, but I decided against the idea. Father's angry eyes were watching my every move. I stood alone in the middle of the room, uncertain what was expected of me.

The candle caught the draught and flickered, casting a shaft of light on Mum, clothes dripping, her beautiful dark hair, now matted, hanging in thick, damp tangles around her slender shoulders, shoeless.

Father, a powerfully built man of 39, standing legs astride at the other end of the room, turned angrily towards me. Eyes narrowing, he glared down and bellowed, "Well kid. Who d'yer wanna live with, me or her?"

I looked up at him with wide, hollow eyes. He straddled the threshold, towering above me in the dim light. I inched back, shivering, nauseated by the stench of stale tobacco on his clothes. Thunder rumbled loudly overhead. At that moment I felt more threatened by Father than the storm.

I turned, pleadingly, towards Mum for a sign of encouragement but saw only a sad, limp figure, motionless. I stood rooted to the spot. My legs would not move. I so wanted to make the right decision. But how could I decide?

Who should I go to: Mum, a pathetic figure in the fading light, or Father, brash and arrogant? What was a five year old supposed to do?

As the grandfather clock struck the hour, rubbing my tired eyes, now desperately wanting to sleep, with renewed inner strength I lunged forward, wrapping my small thin arms around Mother's waist, burying my face in the wet folds of her skirt, trying to hide from the unbelievable nightmare.

The front door slammed.

Silently, Father strode into the storm.

Gone. Out of our lives.

My grandmother, Kitty, and grandfather, Percy Tabor, on honeymoon in Clacton-on-Sea, 17 July 1913

My maternal great grandmother, Katherine Howard

Mum aged three and Auntie Betty aged two

Granddad's bakery shop with bakery and house behind and his fleet of delivery vans at Shenstone, Shenfield

Mr and Mrs R Schrier (Dad and Mum) in 1941,
after my birth, at Shenstone, Shenfield

Granddad and Uncle Gordon, August 1949

Granddad Percy Tabor, 1949

Gran, 49 years old, 1943

Me aged 14 months, Mum holding me, aged 28, Auntie Betty
and Gran at Flat 4, Western Gardens, Brentwood

Me and Susan. Someone has cut out photos of us at the same age and made a collage

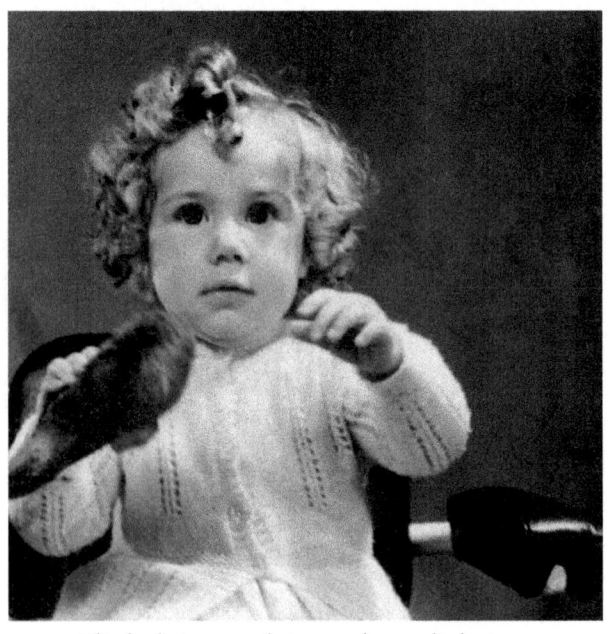

Elizabeth Ann, aged six months, my little sister

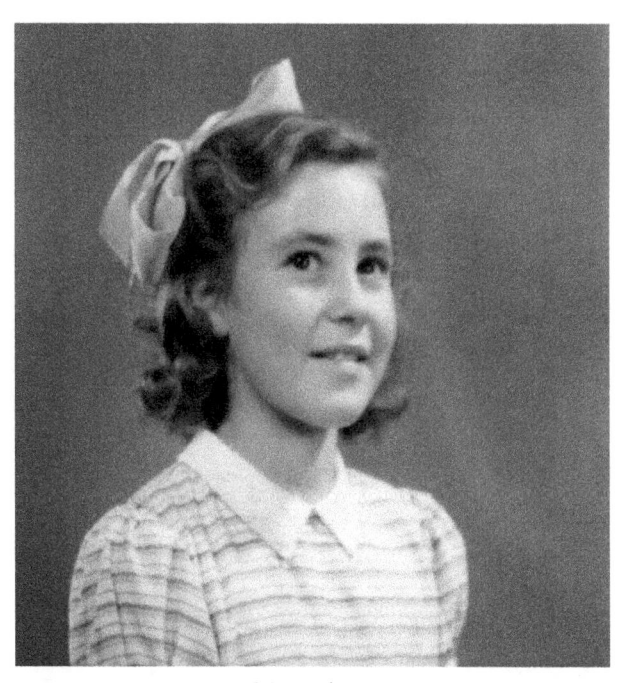

Me aged ten

Me aged seven, Gran and Susan aged five, St Leonards-on-Sea

Chapter 10
Fishy Business

"Where yer goin' kid?" called an inquisitive Mr Kemp one warm mid-June morning, spotting his young neighbour leaving with her bulging tatty brown suitcase, again.

"To live in a fish shop."

"Are you now? 'ope you like it," he remarked between gritted teeth, sucking his pipe, leaning on his garden gate and giving me one of his sympathetic looks. He knew. Everyone knew. Even I knew—now.

"Hate fish. That and swedes." I screwed my nose up just thinking about it.

Jerking my arm, Gran propelled me forward. I didn't know why I had, for once, been pre-informed about being 'put on trial' for another adoption. This time it was only a short bus journey from Gran's flat in Western Gardens. This meant that I could continue my education at the same school, Crescent Council Junior in Crescent Road, which apparently would be within walking distance.

Why did they want to get rid of me?

We arrived at my 'new home' after lunch on a Thursday, half-day closing, in a parade of small shops on a busy main road, not far from Brentwood railway station. The front of the shop appeared neat and clean. I could smell the fresh blue paint.

"This looks nice," Gran chirped cheerily, little realising what lay behind the façade. She rested my suitcase on the pavement, adjusting the red ribbons on my long plaits. A *CLOSED* sign hung in the shop door window. Gran rang the bell anyway.

I stood to attention, fingers crossed behind my back, hoping there was no one home. But seconds later bolts shot across and slowly the heavy wooden door creaked open, and we came face to face with the fishmonger's wife.

"Hello Mrs Wainwright. This is Jacqueline." Gran pushed me forward.

What should I do? Curtsey? Shake hands? I just grinned nervously.

Mrs Wainwright was a short rotund lady with dark hair in curlers under a headscarf set above a round, red jolly face.

"Come on in," grinned the fish lady, "been waiting for you."

"Gran, what's that horrible smell?" I coughed, cupping my hand over my nose.

Before my guardian could answer, Mrs Wainwright piped up.

"Fish! Just fish. You'll have to get used to it if you're going to live here," she chuckled, wiping red hands on a not-too-clean apron.

I don't want to live here.

"Come and meet the family."

As we followed her through the white marble shop into a small room with rough wooden benches, shelves and boxes, the stench grew more pungent. In fact, the further back you went the worse it became. Sliding a heavy oak door across, Mrs Wainwright gestured for us to step into the living room, where her husband, the fishmonger, sat in a corner.

"'Ere's Jacqueline, Vic."

A pair of black bushy eyebrows appeared over the top of a newspaper. Mr Wainwright looked me up and down then carried on reading.

"Don't mind 'im," laughed his wife, her face going even redder. "'e's been up since four. Looks forward to 'is 'alf day's rest."

While Gran and Mrs Wainwright huddled together, plotting my stay, I glanced about me. The living room was oblong shaped with narrow doors at one end leading out on to a small back yard. The once heavily patterned carpet, now badly worn and faded, matched the couch and two armchairs. In the opposite corner sat a gateleg table with a bowl of rotting fruit standing on a paper doily and four odd wooden chairs. On one of the chairs an over-sized tabby cat sat curled up asleep. It opened one eye, stood up with difficulty, turned round and promptly curled up again.

Mrs Wainwright disappeared through a further door into a narrow passageway, beyond which was a small scullery at the rear of the property with stairs to the first floor. A short while later she reappeared, carrying a large wooden tray with three steaming cups of tea of varying shapes and sizes, no saucers, and two glasses of lemonade on it. I was wondering who the second glass was for when a grubby boy, much bigger than me, tumbled into the room carrying an even grubbier football.

"This is our son, George," crowed his mother.

After the introductions and drinks, Gran announced: "Time to go, Mrs Wainwright."

"Right y'are, Mrs Tabor."

A lump rose in my throat as Gran whirled through the shop and out on to the street.

I wondered when I would see her again.

The stench of fish made me gulp. Fearful of throwing up, I reluctantly followed Mrs Wainwright up the dim, narrow bare staircase to the small dark dingy room which, I had been informed, I would be sharing with her son.

"Where's the bathroom?"

"Barfroom?" My new guardian laughed, throwing back her head. "D'yer hear that, Dad? Her ladyship wants a barfroom!"

"We ain't got no barfroom," chipped in George. "The lav's out back."

I stared at them in disbelief. How could Gran send me to such a place? A place with no bathroom. I'd been away from home before but there was always a bathroom. I began to wonder how I would manage.

Mrs Wainwright helped me unpack. I felt nervous with George watching. When he saw my stuffed rabbit in the suitcase, he grabbed it and ran off.

"Bring that back 'ere!" bellowed his mother. "Be'ave yerself or I'll box yer ears."

George was two years older than me. I took an instant dislike to him.

"You be nice to yer new sister, yer 'ear me?" said Mrs Wainwright, tweaking his ear as she left the room.

Conflicting feelings of fear and embarrassment attacked me as I was left alone in the room with George. Big for his ten years, with a mop of thick black hair and large eyes as black as coal, he looked just like his father.

"Just cos you the youngest, don't mean you gets everything."

"What do you mean?"

"Me mum wanted a girl so they got you. But you only adopted," he sniggered, striding out of the door, leaving me alone and bewildered.

Only adopted? Gran had said that 'special people' were adopted. This boy had made it sound like something dirty.

Up on tiptoe, I peered down through the grimy windowpane. The street below was noisy, something I was not used to. On Thursday afternoons most of the shops were closed, but buses stopped outside bringing shoppers back from town. People hurried to and from the railway station, its entrance road almost opposite.

On the other side of the road an ironmonger's, bakery and greengrocer's sat, shutters down today. At the other end stood the Essex Arms public house, on the corner of Bryant Street.

The fish shop was sandwiched between the familiar red and white striped barber's pole protruding from the wall and a newsagent's.

This was my new home. I looked around the cramped room: two small metal beds, green peeling paint, one mine, the other the boy's; an old wooden wardrobe to be shared. I'd never shared a room with a boy before. My stomach fluttered anxiously.

Mrs Wainwright had told me to call her and her husband Mum and Dad. But I'd already got a mum and a dad (somewhere). I don't want any more, I told her.

For tea that evening it was sausages and mash but most days, I was informed, it would be fish. The four of us squeezed round the small table. Mr Wainwright had still not uttered a word to me. In fact, I had learned that he was a man of very few words. He just grunted like a pig and ate like one.

After tea, while helping my new 'mum' with the dishes, she said:

"Your barf night will be Fursday. Mr Wainwright 'as 'is Fridays, so you keep out the scullery then."

The tin bath hung on a nail in the backyard and came in on bath nights. My water was never clean as George got in before me. Other times the tin bath was used for washing fish.

Whenever it rained, a small pool would form on the broken, concreted yard, where fish in various degrees of deterioration, some with heads, some without, bobbed about, their bulging eyes staring into space. Goosebumps would form on my arms as I watched in amazement at the macabre scene. A further three pairs of eyes also watched: the neighbourhood cats with damp fur huddled under an old tarpaulin eyeing their breakfast floating before them.

The following Saturday morning, I accompanied Mr Wainwright and new 'brother' George, as I was repeatedly reminded, to the barber's shop next door, not realising what was in store for me.

I watched with fascination as the barber clipped George's hair, the shorn fluff floating to the floor.

Then it was my turn.

With just a couple of snips, my long dark plaits lay scattered on the shop floor. My reflection in the mirror horrified me. I looked like a boy.

George laughed when I burst into tears.

As usual, his father said nothing.

On our arrival back at the fish shop, Mrs Wainwright could not console me.

"Never mind, it'll soon grow, you'll see. And it won't take long to wash now. You can do it yerself." I remembered the last time my hair was cut short, last time I was sent away, but it was never like this, never this short.

A few weeks later, George went down with measles—good news for me as the doctor told the Wainwrights I must not share a bedroom on account of being exposed to the disease. It was now my turn to laugh at the spotty boy.

My new sleeping quarters was a room at the top of the house, no larger than an oversized broom cupboard, with an old camp bed, cobwebs on the ceiling and peeling walls. But at least I was on my own. No curtain hung on the grimy window, and the light bulb flickered on and off, more off than on, especially when the shilling ran out in the meter. When it rained, water dripped through a hole in the roof, spilling on to the bare floorboards before a white chipped pail was hurriedly placed on the damp patch. In the quietness of that small attic space, external noises echoed. Getting to sleep was often prolonged.

One rainy night, Mr Wainwright brought the pail into my room, stood by my bed and ran a rough hand through my cropped hair. His face inches from mine, I could smell his beery breath, which made me feel faint. He began kissing my forehead then my cheeks then my lips. As he tore the bedclothes back, a call rang out.

"Vic, what yer doin'?" bawled his wife up the stairs. Like a child chastised, the big man quickly left my room, banging the door behind him.

On hearing noises outside, I rushed to the window. Wiping the grime off with the back of my small hand, I peered through the dirty, cracked pane to the street below. People were staggering out of the public house opposite, arms around each other, singing. They sounded happy, a state I was not experiencing lately. Later, in the stillness, I lay listening to the rhythm of the rain spattering the fractured glazed window and drip drip dripping into the pail. Counting the drops, I eventually drifted into a fitful sleep.

A few weeks later, a meeting was arranged with Gran and Mum one Friday after school. Reluctantly, Mrs Wainwright accompanied me, but she was glad her husband had to stay to mind the fish shop, Fridays always being busy.

While waiting for my relatives, I amused myself on the swings, my hawk-eye never leaving the entrance to the playground. As soon as I recognised Gran's hat coming through the gate, I charged towards her and Mum. Mum seemed pleased to see me, giving me a big hug, something I had not experienced lately. Gran seemed distant.

"Now, what's all this I've been hearing?" It felt good to feel a familiar arm around me.

"Let me talk to her, Joan." Gran sounded agitated.

"I want to talk to Mum by myself," I told them, holding my mother's hand tightly.

Gran was revving up for an argument. Then she looked at me and said, "All right, but only five minutes mind you."

Mum and I walked towards the swings. "Now, what's the matter. I hear you haven't been eating and sleeping properly. You'll get ill. We can't have that, can we?"

"Oh my goodness, your hair!" How could she not have noticed? "And what's that smell?"

"Fish. I want to come home, Mum." My pleading brown eyes looked up into her troubled brown ones.

"It's not that simple," she said. "I've got to sign the papers soon."

"But Mum, I hate it here. The smell makes me feel sick all the time, and that boy's horrible to me. He put Rabbit in the freezer."

By now I was really sobbing, my whole thin body shaking. Mum held me tightly against her. We stood silently until my sobs began to subside.

"It would be best for everyone if you stayed with the Wainwrights. You know I'm on these pills and, well, Gran isn't really up to it either. You know we all have to do things we don't want to do sometimes."

"But Mum, I miss you," I sniffed.

We sat on the park bench, relishing the rare moments we were sharing.

"We'll see each other now and again." She brushed tears from my cheeks.

"No, we won't. Not when we go to Australia."

Mum looked as though she had been shot, her face becoming distorted.

"What did you say?"

"I'm going to Australia."

"Over my dead body."

I had never seen Mum move so quickly. She strode back to where Gran and Mrs Wainwright were waiting, pulling me behind her.

"What's all this I hear about you and your family going to Australia?"

Gran butted in. "It's all right, Joan. Everything's been agreed."

Mum was shouting hysterically. "No, it's not all right. I don't like things being done behind my back. You conniving old woman. How could you?"

I looked at my grandmother and mother. I could never remember Mum talking like that, especially to her own mother.

The months of Gran organising and manipulating behind her back had caused my mum's temper to boil over. And I now knew one thing: Mum was on my side.

"I'm not losing her too. Susan and the baby have gone. You are not taking my firstborn. She's coming home with me."

"But you can't…"

"Oh yes I can. Just watch me."

She marched back to the fish shop with her nose in the air and a look of determination on her face, with Gran and Mrs Wainwright tottering behind.

I quickly led the way through the crowded shop, past a startled fishmonger and customers.

"Fetch your things Jackie. We're going home."

Excitedly I ran up the dim narrow staircase, grabbing my few belongings and throwing them into my tatty brown suitcase.

"You can't take 'er away, yer know," shouted Mr Wainwright, wagging a dirty, fishy finger in front of Mum's face.

"Oh yes I can. She's my daughter, not yours."

"But you signed the papers. She's ours."

"You know what you can do with your papers, Mr Wainwright. Come on, Jackie."

Mum grabbed the suitcase and my hand. Holding on tight, I steamed through the amazed, crowded fish shop with Mum. As we passed George, I could not resist poking out my tongue.

But, unbeknown to me, my homecoming would be short-lived.

The adoption society was on the case.

Chapter 11
Chinese Outing

During the first week of the summer holidays, Katherine Tabor, my grandmother, kept a promise and took her young charge to visit the goat lady. The ice-cream parlour in Brentwood High Street now used goats' milk for its frozen delights. Gran had been friends with Mrs Paterson, the goat lady, for years, since school days in fact, and had suggested the idea (she was always full of them).

So, one bright, cloudless Wednesday morning, Gran and I boarded a number seven single-decker bus outside the Odeon in Brentwood High Street to travel the 15 miles to Birch Lane, Margaretting, where the goat lady lived. Some while later, we alighted at Oak Tree Corner, a desolate crossroads in the middle of the countryside with one large oak tree which Gran reckoned to be a least 100 years old (older than her). The rest of the landscape was open green fields, roads with no paths lined by ditches and green hedges which seemed to stretch into the distance in every direction.

"How far's it, Gran?"

I was feeling the heat.

"'Bout half a mile. You can't miss it. It's the only place for miles."

The road was nothing more than a narrow, stony cart track. Pink briar roses and twittering sparrows peppered the hedgerow. Colourful wild flowers, which Gran knew all the names of, and tall white hemlocks adorned the trackside. Passing by I heard crows cawing in the parched, dry buttercup-sprinkled fields and watched a skylark hovering high overhead then suddenly swooping down to earth. On the horizon stood a windmill, and in the distance was a house, the only one for miles around. (Gran was right.) "There it is, Gran!" Excitedly, I rushed forward. Stopping outside the blue painted gate, I read the sign: *Foxgloves.*

It was a bungalow of good size and character set in four or five acres. A large paddock stretched across the rear of the property with several resident galloping horses of differing colours and sizes. To the right, a smaller field housing the goats caught my attention.

Gran marched straight round the back. She obviously knew the way. Suddenly four brown, furry animals hemmed me in, yapping at my feet, and an elderly lady, with neatly permed grey hair poking from under a huge sun hat, appeared.

"Don't be frightened, dear. They won't hurt you. It's just their way of greeting," she croaked.

"These are Choo, Chin and Chow, and this is their mother Ming. She beamed proudly, leaning on her stick. The three younger Pekingese sported dark brown coats, while Ming had fluffy long straight hair in a shiny gold colour with a dark brown, perfectly plumed tail curled to a white tip. I ran my fingers through her coat, looking into her large chocolate-brown button eyes and thinking her the most beautiful dog I had ever seen.

Emily Paterson laughed.

"She likes you, dear." She proceeded to tell us how good Pekes are with children and what an excellent pedigree Ming had, one as long as your arm.

I looked for it but couldn't see it.

"You know her father was at Crufts," she added. "Well, that's enough of that. Come in, dears." The goat lady beckoned us inside, peeling off her sun hat.

"You must be tired after your trek, especially in this heat." Entering by French doors, we found the inside surprisingly cool, the room bright and comfortable looking with velvet drapes, Indian rugs and highly polished dark wooden furniture. (Very different from the utility units back at number 4.) I flopped down on to the inviting red velvet sofa and was quickly surrounded by four wrinkled muzzles, all jostling for attention.

"I expect you'd like a drink, Kitty?"

"Oh, tea for me please Emily," replied Gran, who drank tea no matter the weather.

"And you, my dear?"

I really fancied a glass of milk but thought about the goats. "Ginger pop please," I hastily replied, remembering my ps and qs.

"Ah, that's good." Mrs Paterson looked as though my answer had solved a solution. "I made some only yesterday."

I thought it the best fizzy tingle on my tongue that I had ever tasted, even better than Auntie Myrtle's—and that was admitting something.

"Come now, let's see the goats."

The two refreshed visitors eagerly followed their hostess out to the nearby field. Opening the gate, I noticed the goats were tethered, counting six in total. They were bigger than I had imagined.

The goat lady untied two and handed me the leather ropes. The goats, feeling their new freedom, tugged at the ropes, pulling me with them. They took off. I had no idea that goats were so strong and could run so fast. I tripped but hung on to the two ropes, sliding through buttercups, poppies and grass on my backside until the animals suddenly stopped, much to my relief.

The goats had decided to munch their way into a nearby hedgerow.

Gran soon caught us up. Looking down at me, she ran her hand across her forehead and panted.

"You all right, Jackie? Gave me quite a turn, don't mind saying."

"I'm all right, Gran. It was fun really."

Gran took the ropes as I jumped up, rubbing my rear end. "Oh dear. Just look at your dress, all grass stains." She sighed, raising her eyebrows.

"Don't worry," wheezed Gran's friend, having just caught up. "I've got some stuff that will shift it. In fact, it will shift anything."

Kitty could not tell her granddaughter off, not in front of her benevolent friend, and not when she had offered the special stain remover.

As we walked slowly back towards the bungalow the sun seemed even more intense, and I welcomed a further glass of cold ginger pop. Gran had one of her headaches coming on, so Mrs Paterson made a fresh pot of tea. Most grown-ups seemed to believe this to be a cure for everything. I sank once again into the inviting sofa, apparently none the worse for my experience, with four small, warm bodies nestling up to me.

"Soon be time for their walkies," croaked the dog owner, handing Gran yet another cup of tea. She had obviously said the magic word as eight little ears pricked up, and the dogs quickly slid from my side one after the other, four wagging tails raised high as they headed for the door.

"Come along then," said the goat lady, gathering four differently coloured leads from the hall stand.

"Can I come?" I asked, draining my glass.

"Well, if you feel up to it, dear. You'll be all right, won't you Kitty?"

"Of course. Don't mind me," said my now drowsy grandmother.

Quite close to the bungalow, just behind the gardens, we slowly followed a winding pathway into a small wooded area, the coolness of the shaded trees making a pleasant contrast to the heat of the high sun.

"We come here most mornings and afternoons," the old lady informed me. "It's so handy having this right on our doorstep."

I skipped ahead along the rough path that snaked gently downhill through tall trees, following four wagging tails, passing brambles and wild flowers dotted among dry grass. The further down into the wood we walked, the cooler it seemed. Suddenly the path came to an abrupt end beside a large cornfield displaying red poppies—just like in Monet's painting. The dogs stopped, unsure of which way to go. I realised we had better go back the way we had just come, not knowing how far we had ventured nor how far behind us the goat lady was.

I felt the intensity of the heat as we turned from the bright sunlight back into the wood and began our assent, thankful that the old beech and oak trees formed a natural canopy from the searing sun. Unhurried, I picked wild flowers—red campions, colombines and speedwells, which pleadingly lifted their small faces to me along the path's edge.

Further along the path, I smelt something, something familiar, something like the smell at the Wainwrights but not fish.

Smoke.

The Pekes began whining when they saw flames ahead. Soon panting and throat sore, I found our exit was blocked. I felt frightened and started coughing. Crouching low, cuddling the dogs to me, trying to shield them from the smoke with the skirt of my dress, I undid my belt and threaded it through the four collars so they could not wander off. By now a small breeze had got up, blowing smoke in our direction. Then a faint voice beyond the smokescreen drifted towards me.

"Choo, Chin, Chow, Ming!"

Mrs Paterson. Thank goodness. "We're here!" I yelled as loud as my small voice would allow.

"You all right, dear?" she asked.

"Yes."

"Thank God. The fire brigade's on its way."

It was then that I heard men's voices and the beating of bracken close by.

Firemen and farm labourers emerged, surrounding us, and the next thing I knew I was hoisted into the air and riding piggyback.

"You're safe now, kid," said a kindly fireman.

"What about the dogs?" I coughed, rubbing itchy eyes.

Looking down, I saw four pairs of brown eyes peering from under a pile of dead leaves.

"Well now, would you look at that."

Untying the leash belt, two farmhands scooped up the Pekes, one under each arm, and made their way safely back up the path to the other side of the fire, where the anxious dog lover waited.

"Oh, my darlings," she cooed, hugging and kissing each in turn. "And you, my dear, thank you so much for looking after them." I also received a grateful hug. It made me feel awkward. It was something I was not accustomed to.

The bedraggled bunch made our way up to the bungalow, me still riding piggyback on my saviour, as some men stayed behind to contain and extinguish the remaining fire. The farmer was fearful for his livelihood.

A relieved and happy Mrs Paterson once again put the kettle on to boil for more tea for her army of unexpected visitors, who were swarming the verandah and lawn. They munched through two home-made sponge cakes, which had miraculously appeared.

"You missed all the fun, Gran."

"Fun, young lady!" said one of the firemen standing near me, coming up for air between mouthfuls of cake. "That were no fun. That were a serious business. You and them dogs could have been hurt bad, and the whole wood burnt. And Farmer Hunt, well, he could have lost his cornfield. No, Miss, that weren't no fun."

"I've been asleep," said Gran. "Took one of those headache pills Emily gave me. Proper knocked me out."

We must have all looked a funny bunch, a bit like the Black and White Minstrels, with smoke-streaked blackened faces.

Soon the remaining firefighters arrived at the bungalow after making safe the small wood and securing the cornfield. They too were rewarded with Mrs Paterson's generous hospitality.

All too soon it was time to leave Foxgloves, which made me feel sad. It was also time for the firemen to take their leave, offering Gran and me, much to my delight, a lift on the fire engine to the end of the lane, where we could catch the bus home.

"It's been lovely meeting you, Jackie. It's been quite a day!" said the goat lady, kissing me on the cheek. So much affection! The four little Chinese dogs snuffled around my feet, so I stroked each in turn—Choo, Chin, Chow and Ming.

Yes, it had been quite a day. A wonderful day!

Chapter 12
Summer Holidays

They didn't know what to do with me during the summer holidays. In fact, they didn't know what to do with me at any time. I seemed to be an alien invading their earth, obstructing normal life, banished to another planet. It seemed to be a huge problem: Where should I go? Who should have me? Not that I was naughty, you understand, just lively—and they couldn't handle that.

My tatty old brown suitcase would be pulled out from under my bed, dusted down and stocked with essentials. This particular time, Gran decided that I would spend in the country with my aunt, uncle and four cousins "to recover from my ordeal"—as she put it.

Uncle Ken, who had been in the forces, was a tall, kind man of athletic build with blue twinkling eyes, light brown wavy hair and a moustache. Mum's younger brother, Ken was a twin to Gordon, brown eyes, no moustache, a Cary Grant lookalike.

Uncle Ken had built his own house from the foundations up, every brick and tile lovingly laid, creating a huge detached property to house all six of them. Auntie Myrtle, his wife—short, slim, thick dark hair, warm brown eyes, local brogue—was a true country girl at heart who believed in home cooking and home grown produce, in fact home-made everything. Some things I will always remember in her kitchen: freshly baked bread (a reminder of the aroma from Granddad's bakery) and spiced cakes.

Dinners came with oodles of gravy and puddings with non-lumpy custard. Gran's small allowance would never stretch to such luxuries. She also had an extra mouth to feed, on and off, more off than on. Times were hard, and I was never allowed to forget it.

Not far from my relatives' detached house, 'Shenwood' on Stock Road, Galleywood, stood a quaint old working windmill. This location became a favourite of mine and three of my cousins: Peter aged six, every inch a miniature Uncle Ken minus the moustache; Marilyn, aged five, with thick dark hair, the living image of her mother; and chubby Julie, aged four, with fair hair and blue eyes. John, the youngest, still in a pram, stayed at home. Peter, Marilyn, Julie and I often took home-made food for picnics in the countryside around their home. Mr Shelby, the miller, always covered in a fine white dust, let us watch him weigh and sort flour into hessian bags after it had been ground. I can still smell the dusty floor.

Sitting on the grass outside the mill eating our picnic lunches, we watched the huge sails turning in the warm summer breeze like a giant pterodactyl flapping its wings ready for take-off. Time spent in this peaceful environment filled me with a happiness and contentment which I would always remember and draw strength from, even today.

Across the lane from Uncle Ken's home stood a line of white painted railings enclosing a small racecourse on the common, not far from the church. This was the only racecourse in England to circumnavigate a church. Auntie Myrtle was an active member of St Michael and All Angels. Both she and Uncle Ken are buried there.

My cousins' two collie dogs, Rosie and Charlie, would race around this course with the three of us hard on their heels. This was my Ascot.

Suddenly I am a famous jockey riding my thoroughbred, galloping past ladies under large hats of every colour, shape and size, men in suits and bowlers. First past the finishing post, I proudly steer my glistening brown steed towards the King and Queen to receive my prize, the coveted silver cup. Amid thunderous applause, I bow to their majesties, waving to the cheering crowds, grinning at the press photographers.

Collapsing on the grass, Peter, Marilyn, Julie and I munch juicy red apples from one of Uncle Ken's trees in his small orchard.

Summer days spent with my country cousins always made me feel good inside. The scent of honeysuckle or freshly mowed grass always takes me back there.

During the summer holiday when I was nine, I visited the South Yorkshire countryside, travelling on a coach from London Victoria to Rotherham, where I stayed with Uncle Llew and Aunt Connie.

Llew was Gran's cousin, with short dark hair and of kindly but stern nature. Aunt Connie was stout, buxom and patient. They had no children of their own. Uncle Llew was one of the managers at Maltby colliery, where a Polish labour force resided in village-style accommodation. My relatives had a bungalow onsite, and often the miners would march by waving. I was taken to visit the ruins of Roche Abbey a few miles away, where my Uncle made me a bow and arrow.

As always, I would soak up the fresh air and country smells before returning to the confines of Gran's flat, knowing by now that, within a few days, I would be on my way again to another unknown destination.

Chapter 13
Meeting a Witch

Saturday morning. I loved Saturday mornings especially this one, the last before the start of a new term. Believe it or not, I was looking forward to going back to my primary school, seeing all the familiar faces and participating in playground games. Gran had one of her headaches. I knew to keep out of the way, amusing myself playing quietly in my bedroom. When the knocker sounded, I rushed to the front door.

"It's Mr and Mrs Kemp, Gran," I announced excitedly, wondering what could possibly bring the next-door neighbours to visit us so early, and on a Saturday too. They were smartly dressed. Mr Kemp was even wearing a tie.

"Hi kid. You ready?"

"What for?"

"Oh my God. She doesn't know." Mrs Kemp put a protective arm around me, drawing me close. "You poor little thing."

I stood in the tiny hallway looking up first at Mrs Kemp then at Mr Kemp, totally bewildered. What on earth were they talking about?

"Where's Kitty?" Mrs Kemp pushed by me, hurrying into the front room, where my grandmother lay flat out on the settee.

"You haven't told her! You said you would," she shouted. I had never seen her like this, so upset, so cross. She'd never reacted like this, even when I dropped the eggs on her washing.

Gran rose slowly, brushing her greying hair off her face with the back of her veined hand, "I meant to but you know how it is."

"No, I don't," said Mrs Kemp angrily. I had never seen my kindly neighbour in this state. What was this commotion all about?

My grandmother turned towards me, taking hold of my narrow shoulders.

"Look Jacqueline…"

Oh, I thought, it's got to be something important. She's using my full name.

Then she dropped the bombshell.

"You're going away to residential school again."

You know that feeling when you drop from ten to zero in seconds…

Tears welled up in my eyes. Everything became blurred. My grandmother continued, but I wasn't listening properly. I was learning not to show emotion.

"What with your mother convalescing and me not feeling too good lately, I thought it best."

She disappeared into the bedroom and quickly re-emerged, carrying my tatty old brown suitcase. "It's all packed ready. Look, even Rabbit's in there."

Mr Kemp, snatching the case from Gran, said, "Come on, kid. We'd better get going."

Going where?

Stunned and saddened, I refrained from kissing Gran and obediently followed the Kemps with their noses in the air, through the front door and down the short path, daring to leave the garden gate open behind me.

We must have looked a sorry trio. No one spoke as we trudged to the bus stop at the end of the walkway.

Once again I was on the train (not first class this time) travelling westbound to Liverpool Street, London. I looked out of the window as we steamed past houses and green pastures. I thought of my chickens. No time for goodbyes.

I had been so looking forward to going back to school. I found the lessons interesting and liked learning about different things. I wanted to see my 'friends'. Well, I regarded them as friends even though I never saw them outside school.

Now I had to meet new people, yet again. I supposed I should be used to it. I was growing a thick skin.

Mrs Kemp unravelled a tangled ball of blue wool and started to knit as I watched in fascination, the wooden needles clicking in and out of the yarn.

"I wish I could do that," I sniffed.

"I'll teach you in the holidays if you like," offered Mrs Kemp, kindly patting my small hand.

She offered me the white handkerchief given to her by her husband. "You keep it, kid. Bring it back at Christmas."

Christmas. That seemed light years away. Gran didn't believe in Christmas.

Gripping the hanky in my hand, as though it was a lifeline, I sat huddled in the corner, peering out of yet another carriage window, watching the alien landscape rushing past. Then Mr Kemp encouraged me to play noughts and crosses and hangman and we soon arrived at my unknown destination.

"Where are we?" I asked, looking around at the unfamiliar surroundings.

"Somewhere in Hertfordshire, I think," replied Mr Kemp.

Boarding a green bus, the three of us mounted the stairs to the upper deck. After passing through the town into the countryside, it was soon time to get off.

Crossing the main road, we began walking up a steep hill lined with grass verges and trees, neat gardens fronting neat houses. Once at the top, we passed through large metal gates framed by a shrub border.

Inside, an oval shaped grass area with three large oak trees in the centre was skirted by a narrow road edged with large brick built houses surrounded by more grass, flowers and shrubs. At the far end I noticed a church.

"'Ere we are," announced a puffing Mrs Kemp. "That sure was steep."

A sign near the gate directed us to *Reception*. After pushing open a heavy wooden door with a brass knob, we found ourselves standing on a polished floor in a large square hallway with a few wooden chairs set along one wall. Some paintings depicting country scenes hung from a picture rail. It was not unlike the doctor's surgery back home, only brighter and tidier.

A short time later, a lady about Mum's age, dressed in a dark suit and white blouse and wearing black-rimmed glasses, read my name off a piece of paper she held attached to a buff file.

I stood up and she beckoned me over. "Say goodbye to your parents."

Mr Kemp coughed and stepped forward to enlighten the lady that they were not my parents, explaining why my mother or indeed grandmother had not accompanied me.

"Well, you've delivered her. That's the main thing," said the lady with the file.

Delivered like some sort of parcel, signed for and left. "Sorry kid. See you Christmas," Mr Kemp said gruffly, patting the top of my head. I could tell he was upset by the expression on his face as he strode out of the door.

"Bye dear." His wife gave me a quick hug and, with head bowed, hurried after her husband. I was certain her eyes were moist. Mine lingered after them for a moment, my only link with home now disappearing out of the door. Then I felt the hanky stuffed in my dress pocket, Mr Kemp's hanky.

I squeezed it in the palm of my small hand to give me some sort of courage for whatever lay ahead. Standing alone in the now empty room, my suitcase beside me, I began wondering where I could be going from here.

The lady with the glasses reappeared.

"This way," she said matter of factly, picking up the suitcase. I followed close behind, not wishing to get lost, trying to guess which house I would be staying in. As if reading my thoughts, she suddenly announced, "You will be in number 5."

Walking the short distance from reception to number 5, I looked around, wondering where the other children were.

All the front doors were of different colours.

We entered by a red door into a large hallway with a shiny wooden floor, wide wooden staircase and bannisters rising to the first-floor landing. We then walked into a small anteroom off the hallway with a plaque on the door inscribed with the word *Office*.

"My name is Jane," informed the lady with the glasses clutching my buff file. "And I'm the school secretary here." She went on to tell me that two units of 12 children lived in each house and, as I was a junior, I would be downstairs.

That's good, I thought, as Gran lives in a ground-floor flat.

"Miss Salter is in charge of your unit, so we'll go and meet her, shall we?"

I followed her through a dining room with three large tables, and the lady in question was soon found in the kitchen supervising preparations for the next meal. As soon as I saw her my heart sank, and I wondered what my survival chances would be. Short, dark hair, thin weasel face with long pointed hook nose, dressed completely in black, apart from her apron—a witch if ever I saw one. I looked around, and yes, there was a broomstick standing in the corner. I concluded that this must be her coven, where she was now stirring her poisonous brew in the cauldron, ready for the evening meal.

I made a mental note not to eat that night.

Glaring at me, the witch retied her white wraparound apron strings behind her, obviously annoyed at the interruption. Perhaps it had made her forget her wicked recipe.

"This is Jacqueline," explained Jane, almost apologetically. "She's your new girl. You only have one this term."

"Good," said Miss Salter. "But it's not really my job to show new ones in."

Miss Salter, narrowed eyes, hands on hips, swivelled and stared at Jane. I was convinced she was casting a spell on her.

"Well, I, I suppose on this occasion," said the secretary, "I could possibly do it for you."

We hurriedly left the kitchen and the glaring witch, scurrying along a corridor like two mice. Then we entered a room situated at the front of the house with a big bay window overlooking the green oval: a dormitory (I knew that word now) with five beds, each covered with blue counterpanes, and five lockers standing to attention beside them. Allocated bed number 4, I thought this must be an omen, although I wasn't sure if it was good or bad. Gran's flat was number 4.

Jane deposited my tatty brown suitcase on the floor beside the bed (counterpanes must be kept clean and tidy at all times).

She took her leave of me and left me to unpack and settle in. I felt alone but pushed on with the task in hand. Opening my case, I saw my rabbit nestling on the top.

It went some way to easing my loneliness.

Chapter 14
A Gypsy Wedding

Suddenly uprooted again. You would think I had become accustomed to it. In a way, I suppose I was. It was still pretty daunting for a nine year old.

In class, I found myself sitting next to Rosanna, a Romany gypsy girl. She soon became Rosie to us children and my best friend. We skipped together at playtimes and sat next to each other at school dinners.

"My sister's getting married next week," Rosie announced one morning. "Do you want to come?"

Did I want to go? Of course I did. I had never been to a wedding before. I didn't go to Auntie Betty's, although Susan did. To attend an occasion outside school, which I had never done before, special permission had to be obtained from the powers that be. Fortunately Jane, the resident school secretary, working on my behalf, obtained the required signature. Jane also helped me to find a pretty dress for the occasion and dropped me off at the campsite.

It was a large field with many caravans of varying sizes and colours. Rosie's was a blue one with red shutters and steps. Her mother, a kindly long-dark-haired lady, greeted me with a glass of lemonade. Inside the caravan, a first for me as I had never been in one, was much larger than expected with seating around the sides, a table and bench area, a kitchen and bedrooms.

Soon it was time for the wedding. The weather forecast had predicted rain, so a large tarpaulin had been put up supported by wooden poles driven into the ground and attached to several caravans. Under these were arranged chairs and trestle tables covered with lacy white tablecloths on which various forms of food had been arranged for after the ceremony.

I sat on the grass with Rosie and her cousins. As the music played, Rosie's sister walked in high heels down the floral aisle past us, holding their father's arm. Her wedding outfit was a beautiful long lacy gown, her dark head covered in the same material with flowers and brightly coloured satin ribbons streaming from it around her bare shoulders. When she reached the end of the aisle, the minister greeted everyone and commenced the service. Prayers, blessings and songs were sung, and the couple each cut a small slit in their left wrist with a knife before mingling their blood. Rosie's mum proudly explained that this was a sign of becoming as one in wedlock, and only true Romany gypsies performed the ritual.

Once the ceremony was complete, people danced to music played on fiddles by relatives and tucked into huge amounts of colourful food, most of which I had never seen before. Just as I was getting into the swing of things with these friendly, happy people, Jane appeared, and I reluctantly had to leave the campsite. I'd had an unforgettable time, the like of which I would never experience again.

A few weeks after the wedding, Rosie did not come to school. One of the boys from the top class sidled up to me in the playground, shoved me and said, "Rosie's not coming back yer know."

What was he talking about? I saw Rosie yesterday at school. We sat next to each other in class and played tag in the playground.

"She's left," he continued, seeing the disbelieving expression on my face.

"Me dad says those gypsies were up to no good, so the police have moved them on. So what yer gonna to do now, with yer best friend gone an' all?"

Tears welled in my eyes. At first I refused to believe him, but at registration the teacher announced that

Rosanna had indeed left to move to another school. I wept uncontrollably as the teacher explained that gypsies usually stayed in one place for a short time before moving on. Rosanna would be used to going to a new school.

It was a bit like me, really. I was always off somewhere new.

The only difference, of course, was that every time Rosie moved, her family moved with her.

Chapter 15
'At Last'

Once back at school, following the Christmas holiday, I suffered bouts of homesickness and missed the broken-biscuit tin that Gran kept in the sideboard. Broken biscuits were bought cheaply either from Woolworths, the Co-op or Liptons.

You would think I was used to packing and unpacking my tatty suitcase. I did begin to wonder what it would be like to stay in one place for a period of time like some of the children in my class who lived with their mums, dads, brothers and sisters. I could only imagine feeling 'at home'.

During the recent Christmas break, Gran had mentioned that it might be possible to see Mum, if she were well enough—whatever that meant. As usual, I was never told more than was considered necessary by the adults.

Sister Sarah seemed to take me under her wing, teaching me how to knit, roll up bandages, make hospital corners (which I still do) and keep a diary. She loved to listen to classical music, which I in turn came to appreciate.

The winter of 1951–52 was extremely cold with much ice. At school my third-of-a-pint bottle of milk would freeze, with the silver-foil cap sitting on top of a white, spiky icicle, totally undrinkable. On days like these, the milk crate was put near the stove to thaw. Often it stayed there too long, which resulted in warm milk. Still, better than none.

The playground would ice over quickly that winter, and for our enjoyment we made ice slides. Most games we played turned into competitions. With the ice slides, the person who stayed upright the longest won. Some days we had to wear our coats and even our gloves (if we had any) in class as it was so cold. Schools were never closed, and we still had to go into the playground at break times—no staying inside the buildings.

During the winter, especially on really cold days, I did not like strip washing night and morning (baths were taken only once a week). But I soon got used to it, even without heating.

On Wednesday morning, 6 February 1952, assembly was a rather solemn affair as the headmaster announced that we had a new queen because her dad, King George VI, had died. The teachers seemed upset and the blackboard showed important dates. People said that a younger person taking the throne was a good thing for England—and the world.

At the end of term, my tatty old brown suitcase bulged, and the usual coaches arrived to ferry us home. One girl got off at the same stop as me, but I never did find out her name or where she lived. I was never encouraged to see other children, never having anyone home for tea.

This year Mum's birthday fell on Easter Sunday, 13 April 1952. She would be 38. I made a special card for her and bought a Fry's Chocolate Cream bar from Woolworths in Brentwood High Street. Gran had given me the money, 4d, and I was allowed to go on my own now that I was growing up.

Mum visited for a few hours on Sunday afternoon, and we had cake which Gran had made—a rare treat. Mum didn't stay too long as I had to go with Gran to her Jehovah's Witness meeting in the evening.

All too soon the holiday was over. I was back on the coach, case stowed away in the luggage compartment. The new term was better, with warmer weather—and outdoor life suited me. No more homesickness bouts for me.

By the time the summer holidays came, I felt sad in a way as this particular term had been an enjoyable one with greater friendships forged. Packing our cases, we went our separate ways by coach. I was looking forward to staying in one place for a few weeks, in the flat with Gran.

But when the coach arrived in Brentwood, I couldn't see my grandmother waiting for me. Instead, Mr Kirby was standing there. He explained that Gran was too busy to meet me. I wondered what that meant.

When I arrived at number 4, much activity was in full swing. Boxes, packing cases and old suitcases littered the lounge floor, with Gran buzzing from one room to the next.

"What's happening, Gran?"

"We're moving."

"Moving? Where to?" I couldn't believe it. It seemed as though we had been in the flat forever, well nearly as long as I could remember.

"No more living in this poky flat. I'm moving to a proper house, one with three bedrooms. And you're coming with me, Jacqueline."

That was a relief.

"But what about school?"

"You won't be going back there."

A few days later, a van came to move our few belongings. I felt a little sad as this had been my home, on and off, for a number of years, well ever since starting school at four. At the same time I was excited, Gran even more so.

The chickens didn't come. I had been told they went to a good home before I arrived back from school. Gran said if I liked I could get some more once we had settled in and if space was available. Gran and I sat in the front of the van with Uncle Ken, who was helping us and driving.

The journey seemed to take ages, only because I was so eager to get there. We travelled from Brentwood to Socketts Heath, a suburb of Grays. The house, semi-detached with a hedge and gated front garden and a long back garden, was number 117 Heathview Road. My billet was the box room at the front. Gran had a bigger one next to mine, also at the front. There was a bathroom with a toilet—no going out the back any more—and a third bedroom at the rear plus a hallway, two ground-floor rooms, one with French doors to the garden, and a kitchen. The back garden seemed to go on forever.

When Gran arrived at the property, she sighed.
"At last."
And that's what she called her new home.

Chapter 16
New Beginnings

In that summer holiday back in 1952, I occupied myself by getting familiar with my new surroundings: roads lined with rows of two-storey semi-detached houses of varying designs enclosed by brick walls, hedges and wooden gates. I was left to my own devices, free to roam, spending a lot of time in my own company. This I had not been used to as recently I had been with other children or an adult telling me what to do and when to do it. This new found freedom was a shock to my inquisitive mind but a welcome one. I soon learned to adapt.

While I began my explorations, my grandmother took on a new persona. No more tipples on the sideboard. Instead, colourful china figures and ornaments oversaw the comings and goings. The beautiful grandmother clock stood proudly in its new place with Gran polishing it regularly. She became like a mother hen feathering her nest. Her dresses now were smarter and more colourful. She took to going to the ladies' hairdresser regularly, even treating herself to a perm and blue rinse. She appeared happier, singing around the house and not complaining nor even raising her voice. I was rarely called by my full name.

Gran wanted to consign my tatty old brown suitcase to the dustbin. "You don't need this dirty old thing any more," she surprised me by saying soon after arriving at our new home. "You won't be going anywhere."

Tears dampened my eyes. How could she even think of throwing my beloved suitcase away after all we had been through together? She scrutinised me with her blue eyes and recognised the hurt I was feeling. Unusual for her. "Oh all right, child, but keep it out of my way mind."

This move had certainly mellowed her.

I knew the perfect place for my lovely old suitcase—under my bed. It still contained my few possessions, rather depleted as the years went on, either lost or thrown away. (Not my decision. I was never consulted about these things. They just happened). And, of course, I was used to storing my things in the suitcase. I created a refuge in the box room at the front of the house. I had a whole utility chest now for storage, which I found hard pressed to fill so continued to use my suitcase.

Gran had a flair for needlework—curtains, tablecloths, cushions, you name it she made it. These gave her and the house a new lease of life.

My religious education resumed with intensity. A new Jehovah's Witness hall was soon found in Grays. Thursday and Sunday evenings were spent studying *The Watchtower*. Tuesday evening *Bible* study was undertaken in various homes. Saturday afternoons and Sunday mornings were spent going door-to-door, preaching 'The Word' in and around our new locality.

I could memorise verses, chapters, even whole books from the *Bible*. My King James version was still my constant companion, and I still have it, with various sections of scriptures underlined in blue pen. Although dog-eared and looking the worse for wear, how it survived all these years and through all my upheavals, packing and unpacking, I will never know. Gran would say "it's God's will". I do wonder if there is something in that.

There are only two pieces of my property that have survived over time: the *Bible* and a leather needle case with my name inscribed on it which Mr Kirby made for me and which I still use.

Heathview Road, where my new house stood, is a long road. At one end was Long Lane, which lives up to its name, and at the top end was the main road. We called it Pigg's Corner because a large grocery shop stood there proudly: Pigg & Son. At our end of Heathview Road stood Thurrock isolation hospital, a large brick building, where Mum eventually secured a live-in job, which meant that I was able to see her occasionally. She visited 'At Last' sometimes but didn't stay too long due to her shifts, so I was told. Though I did always notice an atmosphere between her and Gran. As usual, nothing was explained.

One sunny day in August, Gran and I went on a shopping spree, which was virtually unheard of in our house. We took the bus from Pigg's Corner down the hill to Grays, where we visited the Co-op opposite the war memorial at the bottom of the High Street. The trip was for my benefit, so I was told, to fit me out for a school uniform for my new school: one grey pleated skirt, two long-sleeved white blouses, one navy cardigan, three pairs of knee-length socks, one pair of sensible brown outdoor shoes, which would have to last so Gran said, the usual supply of underwear, a school blazer and a PE kit comprising shirt, shorts and plimsolls. I had never had so many new clothes all at once.

A network of wires ran across the ceiling in the draper's department with small metal boxes on pulleys which the sales assistants used to transport payment of goods to a central cashier sitting in a control box. It reminded me of a toy train set. I watched in fascination as the small bell rang and the money travelled along its small cables.

I was proud of my new uniform and thought how smart and grown-up I looked. The school year couldn't come quickly enough for me. My new school was a girls' secondary modern in Bridge Road, Grays, opposite Grays Park. The boys' school was next door.

Girls only. This was going to be quite an experience for me. On my first day I felt excited and a little apprehensive. I walked from 'At Last' to Park School, which took me nearly half an hour. This was no problem for me; I had been used to walking to school since the age of six, so my legs were strong and well developed.

I was quite calm as I knew I was not staying overnight but going back to 'At Last', to my own little bedroom after school. This was a first for many years.

I was put in a class with 30 other girls of all shapes and sizes, given a timetable for weekly lessons and allocated a locker for my PE gear. My form teacher looked about Mum's age. With fair hair in a bun, she was of medium height and stature, a kind looking lady with sparkling blue eyes and a soft voice.

Sitting at the back of the room, looking around the class at the other girls, I suddenly felt a wave of nausea sweep over me. I was afraid and reluctant to speak to anyone. I felt like an outsider. They all seemed to know one another and were chatting and laughing.

One thing I had learned since going away so often was not to trust anyone except myself. It was easier to keep people out, to compartmentalise things and keep others at arm's length. These girls frightened me, but I knew only too well how to put on a brave face. After all, I'd had plenty of practise.

The subjects were interesting, and I wanted to learn the variety on offer. I particularly enjoyed history and geography, English, needlework and art (though I was not too good at the latter). Sport became my favourite. I excelled in athletics, field and track and was chosen for the tennis team, which practiced across the road in Grays Park.

Chapter 17

New Found Freedom

My love of the printed word started at an early age: reading, writing, crosswords, anything that presented a challenge. Fortunately, my grandmother had the same interest, having the *Daily Express* newspaper delivered to 'At Last' each morning.

In the spring of 1953, close to my twelfth birthday, the *Daily Express* ran a competition asking readers to write a witty poem. The prize was tickets for the Australia versus Essex cricket match. Unfortunately, I do not recall my ditty, written on a plain white postcard, but do remember, to my surprise, that it was good enough to win two tickets for the match to be held in Southchurch Park, Southend-on-Sea.

I decided to treat Mum. It was a warm, sunny August day, and it didn't matter that Australia beat Essex over three days by an innings and 212 runs. We just enjoyed our day out, eating our picnic lunch, laughing and simply being together. It was a good feeling being with Mum, just like it was for any other mother and daughter I imagined. Not an experience I had too often.

Aged 11, I was growing up fast according to some people. My body and mind certainly noticed changes during this year. By moving to 'At Last' I was finally able to settle in one place. But for how long?

My new found freedom often took me to the local playing fields at Blackshots, where I could walk on my own without escorts or anyone to annoy me. I also visited Hangman's Wood at Dane's Corner near Blackshots. I began to find this time comforting and calming and didn't mind being in my own company. Well, I had been alone all my life, so it seemed, one way or another.

At school, we had a weekly timetable for various subjects and teachers. Mine were maths with algebra and logarithms, English, history, geography, domestic science, needlework and PE. I excelled in all except maths.

My religious education became more intense too. Tuesday evening *Bible* classes were held in various people's homes, often Gran's. Thursday evenings were Kingdom Hall meetings. Saturday afternoons and Sunday mornings were spent going door to door, preaching The Word and selling *The Watchtower*. I never experienced going to anyone else's house and never socialised in that way. The only people I associated with were Gran's religious acquaintances and occasionally some family members. Gran didn't appear to have friends and nor did I, though I did sometimes miss the company of the children from boarding school. But only sometimes.

The summer holidays seemed endless and my new freedom somewhat daunting, but as the days passed I soon worked things out by planning what to do and when. This would stand me in good stead throughout my life.

During sunny summer months, I would often accompany Gran pea picking not too far from our house, a bike ride along Long Lane. Gran always took a picnic, which was eaten sitting on the grass in the pea field. Picking the pea pods from vines eventually made my hands red and sore and blistery. We were expected to fill large brown hessian sacks, and Gran was paid a few shillings per sack after they were weighed. (One shilling being 12 pence, 20 shillings one pound note—not coins.) Of course, I never knew the amount.

Gran wasn't the only adult I shared this activity with, although with Mum it was apples that we picked, again by hand, putting them gently into wooden crates so that they wouldn't bruise. I did enjoy eating the juicy red ones. It was a bit of extra money for Mum.

Near Pigg's Corner, at the top of Heathview Road, at the junction where the main road went down into Grays, stood a parade of shops, including a newsagent where I got a job as a paper girl delivering daily papers close to my road. I had to get up early, 6am, but this job gave me a regular income, which I often spent on records and magazines.

Sometimes I would sail across the Thames by ferry boat from Grays to Gravesend in Kent, where I visited an open-air swimming pool. I loved the smell of the saltwater and the sea breeze.

Sports days at Grays Park School were memorable for me as I enjoyed competing in all the disciplines. On one occasion at inter-school sports, during the hurdle final, I tripped and sprained both ankles and was sent home in a taxi. My paper round suffered for a few weeks, but the newsagent was sympathetic and gave me the job of marking up the papers for the delivery boys and girls. That was a good thing as I was still earning money. The only bad thing was that I had to be at the shop by six in the morning. I soon adapted.

Mum now lived in and worked in the hospital in Long Lane at the end of Heathview Road, but I didn't see her much due to her shift times. She wasn't there for long. She moved to Brentwood Hospital on Shenfield Road and worked as an orderly. I was 14 by then.

Chapter 18
Kennylands

Nearing the end of the summer holidays in August 1955, aged 14, excitement gripped me at the thought of returning to my senior school.

I stared at my uniform with pride, looking forward to wearing it again. I finally felt I belonged somewhere. Happiness picked me up and gave me a big hug.

"You won't be needing that." Gran strode into my bedroom and prised me and my happiness apart.

"W-w-what?" I stammered.

"You're going to a new school."

"But…"

"No buts about it, child. It's all arranged."

And that was that. Tears stung my eyes. Don't cry. It's a sign of weakness.

I couldn't help it. I collapsed on my bed, sobbing. Please God don't let this happen. It just can't happen. I'd had three glorious, continuous years at Park Secondary Modern School. I was so looking forward to the new term. I had even earned a place on the netball team, athletics squad and tennis team. I'd made some friends, though I still didn't fully trust anyone. Perhaps that would come in time. My school reports were good. The teachers seemed to like me and I them.

Yet, again, here I was being uprooted. No one consulted me. No one mentioned it.

I just had to know why. Why now? I was due to leave school next summer after my exams, when I would be 15.

The following morning after breakfast, porridge and the *Yearbook* and *Bible* reading, I dared to tackle Gran, who explained that I would be continuing my education at a school in Berkshire, where I would learn shorthand and typing as I would need to get a proper job after leaving school. She informed me that the coach would be leaving the following morning. No time for goodbyes, not even to Prince, the friendly black-and-white collie next door.

So, with a heavy heart, I retrieved my old brown tatty suitcase from under my bed, shook the dust off and began the arduous task of packing a few clothes. No uniform required this time, just sensible attire: three long-sleeved white blouses, one grey skirt, one laundry bag, brown lace-up shoes, three pairs of knee-length white socks, plimsolls, dressing gown and slippers.

The following morning, after the devastating news of my sudden departure—yet again with all the essentials stuffed into my bulging suitcase, my stomach knotted up as I slowly walked along the road and waited for the coach at Pigg's Corner. It was September 1955. For all I cared I could have been going to the other side of the world. Gran and I waited in silence until the coach arrived. The only thing she said was that she would see me at the end of term, Christmas, three-and-a-half months away. Then she was gone. No hug. No wave. Nothing. I would like to think she felt guilty.

As I mounted the coach steps in a dream, I wondered how I would survive. With heavy legs, I climbed into the coach. My spirits were soon uplifted as chattering, cheerful faces of boys and girls came into view. Perhaps this was going to be all right after all.

My destination was Kennylands, a co-educational college situated in Sonning Common near Reading, in the heart of the Berkshire countryside. A small village, Sonning Common seemed miles from anywhere and indeed was. At Kennylands I was put in a ten-bed dormitory in a long, army-style hut, possessions by my bedside stacked in a locker/cupboard. All beds were metal and painted white with green counterpanes. I soon slipped into the routine of shared living again. Old habits and routines die hard. A couple of girls became my friends, Jill and Ann. Jill was short and plump with dark blonde shortish hair and blue eyes. Ann was tall and thin, like me, with brown hair and brown eyes.

I promptly discovered that shorthand and typing were not on the curriculum. My heart sank. Slipping into a deep depression, I wanted to go home but was not permitted to leave and told I had to make the best of a bad job. As before, I seemed drawn towards sickbay, where I found solace, a safe retreat. I am sure Sister Joan understood my feelings of immense disappointment and mental turmoil. But I was growing stronger and more emotionally able to cope with situations. I believed things could only get better.

The headmaster's wife, a petite, dark-haired kind but strict lady and a trained Victor Silvester dancer, soon got us learning the waltz, quickstep and foxtrot with dances held every Saturday evening. I quickly mastered the steps and loved swaying to the infectious music and dancing with the boys. (One advantage of a co-ed.)

After the Christmas holiday, my interest turned to reading newspapers and scanning the job columns. I knew that I wanted to work in London and be a journalist. It sounded so grown-up and romantic. I practised writing job applications for when I could apply for real. I also took my metal roller skates with leather toe-caps back with me and enjoyed whizzing around the tarmac paths that surrounded the buildings at Kennylands.

During this year of my education, I enlisted with a pen pal club advertised in a London newspaper. I corresponded with several girls of my age, one a Japanese girl whose family had been caught up in the Nagasaki bombing during the summer of 1945. She sent me a pair of painted wooden dolls, which I still have. The other was an Italian girl who lived near the mountains and spent her holidays skiing. Also, Uncle Gordon had a lady friend in Germany. He often sent her parcels of coffee, and I regularly wrote to her daughter, Uta. I did look forward to receiving my blue airmail envelopes with foreign stamps.

The pungent smell of vinegar always takes me back to Kennylands, where us girls had to wash our hair every Friday lunchtime. Washing facilities were situated in a long hut with many basins. There we had to rinse our hair in vinegar (to make it shine). The boys always sniggered and made fun of us back in class, holding their noses.

During that period of my life, I developed a fondness for coffee. Camp coffee came in screw-top glass bottles, a thick, dark, strong liquid poured into cold milk. Pure nectar. One bottle lasted for ages.

I met my first boyfriend at boarding school, Jimmy White—a good athlete and a decent dancing partner and not bad looking. I do not remember feeling homesick like some of the others. Maybe I had become immune.

During the Christmas holidays of 1955, as Mum was still working at Brentwood Hospital, where she had a room of her own, she was granted permission for me to stay with her for one night only. It was the night of the annual staff Christmas party. I loved the live band and danced all evening. Well, I could now, couldn't I? I was even allowed to play drums with the band for the Jim Lowe hit 'Green Door'.

Music I found soothing and bought records when I could afford to, playing them on Uncle Gordon's radiogram. We were getting modern at 'At Last'. Songs from 1956 included 'Just Walkin' in the Rain' by Johnnie Ray, 'Singing the Blues' by Guy Mitchell and 'Que Sera, Sera' by Doris Day. Sometimes, when I had some extra cash, I would buy sheet music and learn the words of my favourite songs. But that wasn't very often.

I had been told that my father's family were related to Joop Schrier, who played piano with the

Dutch Swing College Band, founded in May 1945. They played traditional Dixieland music, which I loved and still do.

My time at boarding school ended in July 1956, when I was 15. Any friendships formed did not survive beyond that summer, but I did continue writing to my pen pals for a while.

After stuffing my old suitcase with my few belongings, I headed back by coach for the last time to Pigg's Corner, Little Thurrock, where Gran met me.

I had left without any qualifications.

Chapter 19
The Elms

In my mind the previous year spent at Kennylands was unproductive and a waste of time. I hadn't learned shorthand and typing, which I had been expected to do, though I did embrace one new skill which became a grounding for adulthood: dancing.

My grandmother insisted I learn a trade to enable me to support myself. She wanted me to be a hairdresser. I couldn't see the point of standing on my legs all day in one spot in a hot, stuffy room, chatting to old ladies having their blue rinses and perms.

Without consulting me, which was normal, she enrolled me in a further education course (for 15 to 16 year olds only) for one year at The Elms in Grays, situated at the top of Bridge Road. Shorthand

and typing were definitely on the timetable along with bookkeeping, commerce and English, all skills deemed necessary for an office job. Exams were compulsory at the end of the summer term the following June.

At least this time I was informed in advance of my destination, but only by a few days, and I would continue living with Gran at 'At Last'. So I entered my final year of formal education. Returning home, as I now called number 177 Heathview Road, my old bedroom seemed smaller but welcoming nonetheless. The only real surprise was that Uncle Gordon, twin of Uncle Ken and a bachelor, had moved in during the time I was away and occupied the larger rear bedroom, which I had hoped to have. Uncle Gordon was a master baker by trade like his father, my grandfather, and worked as a delivery man, driving an electric van for the Grays Co-op bakery. We had fresh bread and rolls every day.

My green Raleigh bike with the wicker basket on the front, which I had rescued from the Tilbury floods of 1953 for £2.10s, was still usable and enabled me to travel to college cheaply and quickly. Uncle Gordon taught me how to mend a puncture and generally maintain the brakes, chain, wheels etc. Also, I would give my bike a weekly wash by turning it upside down in the backyard. I was really proud of it once it gleamed, especially the chrome work.

Before commencing my course at The Elms, on one of my trips to Grays High Street, I saw a notice in the Co-op window: *Saturday Girl Wanted*. Good news. Just what I wanted and needed—pocket money.

I attended the interview in a smart striped blue dress, kitten heels and no white socks and was ushered into a small office at the back of the store by a dark-haired, red-faced jovial lady—the manageress. She wore a brown suit, glasses and a moustache. Of course, I got the job. There was no competition in those days. I loved the smell of the new material and silk stockings in the draper's department, where I worked, and watching the overhead pulleys. Having my own money to spend had become a reality. I could now afford to get the bus to work every Saturday.

The Elms, a large old brick manor-style house situated among trees on a hill with a steep driveway contained many rooms on two floors accessed by a large wide wooden staircase.

The students, boys and girls all aged 15 to 16, were treated as young adults and expected to behave as such. Uniform was not compulsory, but we were expected to wear something 'suitable'.

My interest in fashion was beginning to germinate, and Gran bought me some new clothes from the Co-op in Grays High Street: skirts, cardigans and button-up blouses.

There were mixed classes, although more girls than boys attended. I still wanted to be a journalist. I just loved reading and the written word, and following news stories fascinated me.

At The Elms I learned to use a metal Remington typewriter and mastered touch typing, with covered hands.

I also took to Pitman's shorthand like a duck to water. At first the squiggles were an enigma, but after a couple of weeks the penny dropped. I soon became proficient in both, maintaining good speeds each week. According to our teachers, City employers required shorthand speeds of at least 80 words per minute and typing 50 to 60 was acceptable.

I also enjoyed the English and commerce but was not too enthusiastic about the bookkeeping. Numbers were not really my thing and still aren't.

Lunchtimes were most enjoyable. We students found an old wind-up gramophone stored in a cupboard. We played records and danced to Bill Haley's 'Rock Around the Clock', Frankie Lymon and the Teenagers' 'Why do Fools Fall in Love?' (my contribution) and Elvis Presley, of course.

Weather permitting, we frequented Grays Park just down the road from the college—opposite my old secondary modern school—to eat our lunches. All the students got on well, but as far as I was concerned no firm friendships were forged. I still did not trust my feelings towards others, adults included. Though I was learning.

However, I did correspond with a male Jehovah's Witness who lived in Dunmow and rode a motorbike. I had met him at a convention. Malcolm visited a few times. We received no encouragement from Gran and I was forbidden to ride pillion, which resulted in my interest waning. Also I had never heard of Dunmow. It sounded alien to me.

At another JW convention, I became friendly with a boy called John, three years older than me. Gran didn't seem to mind this time (no motorbike) but again gave me no encouragement.

We visited each other's Kingdom Halls on Sundays, and once his parents invited me to their council house in Dagenham.

Opposite our house, number 177 in Heathview Road, were a pair of identical, semi-detached mock-Tudor-style houses. A young man named Peter, a keen photographer, lived in one. He thought I was photogenic (I didn't have any spots) and wanted me to pose (with clothes on, I might add). Gran consented, on the condition that he came to our house, which proved difficult for him because of lighting and equipment, but we were both pleased with the results. In fact, he was so pleased with his work that he entered a local competition and won a prize.

During my year at The Elms, Mum visited a few times. On one occasion, we went to the Regal cinema off Grays High Street to see *Footsteps in the Fog* starring Stewart Granger and Jean Simmons in 1955. (Quite scary.) *Reach for the Sky* with Kenneth More and Murial Pavlow was another film we saw and enjoyed. I had just the one holiday with Mum. Gran treated us to a caravan for a week in Clacton. I don't think we had any disagreements.

Film going was also a solitary pursuit. I loved seeing films at the Odeon, Ritz and the State, all situated in Grays, and would buy the *Picturegoer,* a weekly magazine, for 4d. *High Society* with Grace Kelly and Frank Sinatra was a favourite as well as *Bus Stop* with Marilyn Monroe. I liked to buy the glossy black-and-white photographs of some of my favourite stars.

Allotments reverted back to ordinary people after World War II, when they had been commandeered for national food production. People grew their own vegetables and fruit in wartime. These had not been rationed but were in limited supply. Gran was no exception. She loved her garden and grew various flowers, though mainly red geraniums in terracotta pots. Also in her garden flourished many edibles such as potatoes, runner beans, strawberries, raspberries and blackberries. To earn pocket money (I was never given it) I filled one-pound glass jam jars with blackberries and sold them for a few pennies to regular customers in the streets near our house. The jam jars were returnable to JW Pigg & Sons store at Pigg's Corner for a halfpenny.

Recycling is not a new concept.

Chapter 20
New Horizons

Spring 1957, just before my sixteenth birthday, Sunday 28 April, Gran became ill. It was a really bad day. Yet again nobody explained the cause, but it resulted in her being admitted to hospital, where she passed away eight days later, on 6 May 1957. I now know that it was ovarian cancer—the Big C, which was never spoken of in those days.

I don't remember feeling any emotions, but I must have, mustn't I? I do know I felt alone. Gran's cremation and internment were held at Croydon crematorium a few weeks after her passing and her ashes scattered with a few words from her eldest son, Uncle Jack, a bank manager. His wife Margaret was a teacher.

About a week after her funeral, six of Gran's seven children swooped on 'At Last' like a swarm of locusts. I watched in stunned disbelief as the house was stripped virtually bare and with sadness as the beautiful wooden grandmother clock was loaded into the back of one of their cars. So much for Gran's promise that it would be mine one day. I was left with nothing to remind me of her but pleased that they did not take my bed.

It was the worst day of my life.

I felt shattered. Numb.

There was more bad news to come. As Gran's house was rented, the lease terminated, and I was shocked when, just after the funeral, Uncle Gordon informed me that I had to move out.

Where to? No one offered me a room, not friends nor family. No one was prepared to take me in.

Was I that bad? I was just 16 with no experience of this kind of thing. Gran had always made decisions for me.

With a heavy heart, I set about to resolve my homeless predicament. Luckily, I managed to secure a temporary roof over my head with a fellow student from The Elms and her family, who kindly offered me a room for a few weeks to see me through my exams. Her father was a teacher at Palmers College, Chadwell Road, Grays. It was a relief. I was about to panic about my forthcoming exams, which were in four weeks and which I could not afford to miss, having put so much energy into mastering the subjects. I really needed to pass to enable me to get a job and support myself—as obviously no one else was going to, no fairy godmother or grandmother.

Without any help, assistance, advice or encouragement from anyone, and left to my own devices, I began the Herculean task of revising. Along the way, I had developed a knack of emptying my mind of unwanted thoughts, which stood me in good stead at this stage. I found the exams nerve-racking but am happy to say that my efforts did not go unrewarded and I passed in all subjects: shorthand typing, English, commerce and even bookkeeping (to my surprise) in the June of that year, 1957.

Jobs were plentiful in the mid 1950s. You saw a job, you got it; there was no competition. With my desire to work in newspapers, I regularly scanned the media adverts. To my delight I easily secured a position as a junior trainee reporter on the weekly Southend-on-Sea newspaper. But my hopes were immediately dashed due to Gran's passing and my change in circumstances. Sadly, I could not follow my dream.

However, as office jobs in London were also abundant, I was able to secure a job in my second choice of work, with Bryce, Robarts & Company, a small family run importer of Italian marble situated in Creechurch Lane EC3 in the City of London, not far from Fenchurch Street station.

I was to be a junior shorthand typist, which required me to take dictation and type up letters. If a mistake was made, the whole letter had to be retyped. One day I accompanied Mr Mott, the import manager, who lived in a prefab in the Stratford area, to the Royal London docks, where a vessel had shipped in Vetrum vitreous Italian marble tiles destined for the walls of the Dartford Tunnel, due to open in 1963. My pay was the princely sum of £6.50 per week. That would be six one pound notes and one ten shilling note in a little buff envelope every Friday.

Mine. All mine. I was going to be rich! Well, we can all dream.

After my exams and celebrations with the other students at The Elms, I had to move on—yet again— as my lodgings were only temporary, this time with my old suitcase and a cardboard box tied with string. I realised I was accumulating too many possessions. I moved to Dagenham, to my boyfriend John's parents' house, and shared a bedroom with his sister, Barbara, who was getting married the following month. I liked her. She was kind to me, like a big sister in a way. But like most things in my life, this did not last. A few months later I gave his ring back. No hard feelings. I was far too young, at 16, to be engaged, just a child really, I was told. I moved out—again—taking my old suitcase containing my few possessions with me. I had got packing and moving down to a fine art by then.

Fortunately, I was offered a room in a lady's house just around the corner, where I often watched a TV programme called *Oh Boy!* after returning by train from my job in London. She was a kind lady, motherly. She made me some beautiful dresses, one in a pretty yellow silky material.

I missed riding my bike so Mr Thomas, my boss, who lived in Surrey, married to the managing director's daughter, kindly signed a hire purchase agreement for me to buy a Raleigh Pink Witch, as advertised by Jackie Collins.

Jackie Collins got a Pink Witch,
Pink Witch, Pink Witch,
Jackie Collins got a Pink Witch

This ditty was sung in the advert with the young starlet riding the bike. I wanted to be just like her.

The bike was only available in pink and fitted with blue mudguards, a white saddle bag, mirrors and a lipstick holder.

A really grown-up model it was. A dream machine.

At least my job in the City seemed stable. I progressed well and was soon promoted to secretary to a director, Mr Thomas, albeit junior one—but then so was I.

My childhood had been a series of dramatic changes. I never could be sure where I would be from one day to the next. And since my grandmother's passing, my life had taken one more dramatic change of direction. The difference this time was that I was no longer a child but a confident young woman, a survivor.

And I knew life would be fine.